BUSHCRAFT

A FAMILY GUIDE

JOHN BOE &
OWEN SENIOR

Fun and Adventure
in the Great Outdoors

Vie Books is an imprint of Summersdale Publishers Ltd

Summersdale Publishers Ltd
46 West Street
Chichester
West Sussex
PO19 1RP
UK

www.summersdale.com

Printed and bound in the Czech Republic

ISBN: 978-1-84953-741-4

Substantial discounts on bulk quantities of Summersdale books are available to corporations, professional associations and other organisations. For details contact Nicky Douglas by telephone: +44 (0) 1243 756902, fax: +44 (0) 1243 786300 or email: nicky@summersdale.com.

John: *On my part I would like to dedicate this book to my wife Kate, my rock and driving force, and Zack, my crazy little adventurer and bushcraft munchkin.*
In loving memory of Stella Hornby, my grandma, you are sorely missed x

Owen: *To the Fendleys – for normality and laughter*

DISCLAIMER

Neither the authors nor the publisher can be held responsible for any loss or claim arising out of the use, or misuse, of the suggestions made herein. Laws and regulations do change, so the reader should seek up-to-date professional advice on any such issues.

The intent of the authors is only to offer information of a general nature to help you introduce your family to bushcraft.

Above all, the safety of you, your family, and those around you is of paramount importance when practising bushcraft. This should be your priority at all times.

CONTENTS

ABOUT THE AUTHORS

JOHN BOE

John Boe has been interested in bushcraft for much of his life, attending his first survival course as a Scout at age 12. John joined the armed forces at age 18, and undertook expeditions to the Austrian Alps, the Kuwaiti desert, Norway and the Highlands of Scotland.

In 2008, John left the forces and settled in Dorset with his family, where he became the founder and owner of Wildways Bushcraft, where he takes genuine pleasure in passing on his love of bushcraft by teaching practical and adaptable survival skills.

OWEN SENIOR

Owen Senior grew up in Dorset and loves being in the woods with his dogs, exploring awesome places and jumping in the sea.

He's been lucky enough to work in the great outdoors, helping people have adventures, for many years and is happiest when he is teaching bushcraft, is a little bit grubby and smells of woodsmoke.

Owen is currently head of bushcraft at Land & Wave and is a British Bushcraft Association instructor assessor, helping a lot of outdoor companies train their staff in all things bushcraft.

INTRODUCTION

❝ Our species is not designed to sit slouched on a sofa staring at a screen ❞

Bushcraft is a strange and wonderful label that covers an eclectic mix of exciting, interesting, noisy, muddy, quiet, tiring, but always outdoor activities. For us, bushcraft is being outdoors with a purpose, enjoying the landscape with something to keep the eyes and hands occupied while the brain is let loose, just to be.

Bushcraft and adventure should never, ever, be about lots of expensive equipment, compulsory leather hats or way too much camouflage clothing. Bushcraft, foraging, journeying and woodland skills are about sharing an experience that is amplified by the environment and remembered because of the people you were with.

Bushcraft is often free and always cheap, and there are few better ways to spend time with your family without spending loads of cash.

The best experiences, especially the best outdoor experiences, are those that are shared with friends and family.

The best way to enjoy bushcraft is to do so safely, being careful and cautious at all times.

- Use sharp tools as they are intended and always supervise children carefully.

- Fires can be very damaging to the landscape; make sure all fires are completely out and the area cleared of debris before leaving any site.

- Hygiene is really important; especially when preparing food, wash hands and utensils often – even when you're out in the woods.

Bushcraft, adventure, getting dirty, stinking of woodsmoke, exploring, hunting, camping, foraging, hiking, scrumping – all those things that together encompass 'being outdoors' are important for human beings to do. Our species is not designed to sit slouched on a sofa staring at a screen; *Homo sapiens* have spent most of the last two hundred thousand years outdoors and we are only the most recent species of hominids. That outdoor evolution over millions of years has made us the wonderful, innovative, creative animal that we are today.

I wonder how many more years of smartphones, tablets and game consoles it will take for us to start devolving?

The contents of this book are simply a few ideas that we hope you'll try. We really, really hope that you'll get the 'bug' and start spending more and more time outside with the people you love. Perhaps you can persuade your friends to do the same; more people getting outside means more knowledge, enthusiasm and energy for all the wonderful things you can do in the great outdoors.

We hate rules, we really do, but there needs to be one rule out there in the woods or wherever else your journey takes you. No phones (except for emergencies). No iPods. No tablets.

Just friends, family, food, woodsmoke, dirt and laughter.

There is a pleasure in the pathless woods;

There is a rapture on the lonely shore,

There is society where none intrudes,

By the deep Sea, and music in its roar.

I love not Man the less, but Nature more.

Lord Bryon, *Childe Harold's Pilgrimage*

A QUICK WORD ABOUT THE LAW

 Always ask permission of a landowner before entering their private property

ENJOYING THE LANDSCAPE

Respect landowners' property and always ask permission of a landowner before entering their private property. Although, technically trespassing is not a criminal offence, it can be construed as a civil wrong. You will need the landowner's permission if you intend to dig up plants to access the roots, hunt or stay out overnight.

The best way to get a landowner's permission is to ask really nicely – writing an email or letter can get great results.

Good ways to find out who owns a piece of land is to ask around the local area or email likely organisations like the National Trust, the Forestry Commission or farms. Facebook groups and internet forums can also be very helpful.

UK KNIFE LAW

UK knife law can appear a little confusing and complicated.

Should the police, or anyone else for that matter, question your need to carry a knife you will need to prove that you are carrying that knife for a genuine reason.

Bushcraft is a genuine reason for carrying a knife in the woods.

If you take any knife into an environment where you have no reason or justification to carry it then you can be prosecuted.

For example, if you stop to pick up some supplies at the supermarket prior to a trip to the woods then make sure that you have removed your knife from your belt.

When a knife is not being used it must be stored correctly, safely and discreetly.

Carrying a knife on your belt or in your pocket and using it for bushcraft is absolutely legal. When you're travelling to and from any area that you intend to use for bushcraft make sure all your sharp tools are stored in your rucksack, car or kit bag.

For more information we recommend you visit www.gov.uk/buying-carrying-knives.

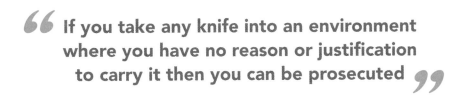

If you take any knife into an environment where you have no reason or justification to carry it then you can be prosecuted

EQUIPMENT

66 **Bushcraft is all about using what nature provides and working with the seasons in order to make yourselves comfortable** 99

You've decided to get your tribe outside and into bushcraft – excellent! Being in the great outdoors with family and friends cannot be beaten.

- **So what kit are you going to need?**

- **Is it going to be expensive?**

- **Where can you get it?**

In brief, the answers to these questions are: not a lot, no and anywhere you like.

Bushcraft is all about using what nature provides and working with the seasons in order to make yourselves comfortable. So don't panic, it's not going to cost an arm and a leg, unless you're a gear junkie and you want it to!

THE BASICS

Clothes – Suitable for the time of year. If you or the kids get cold then that's the day over and they won't want to go out again. A good, warm coat is a must and fleece-lined trousers are a bonus in the winter, but long johns are just as good. Waterproof coats and trousers are a necessity in the UK, we take ours even when it's wall-to-wall sunshine, just in case. Don't forget the basics of hats, gloves and decent socks – nobody likes cold toes!

Knife – For most of the activities in this book you are going to need a knife. A great and inexpensive place to start is the Mora Clipper as it is perfect for bushcraft and wood working.

Saw – An example of an inexpensive and efficient saw is the Bahco Laplander. It is basically a folding pruning saw that cuts on both the push and pull strokes making your life a lot easier when it comes to crafting things with your family.

First aid kit – It is always good practice to take a small first aid kit with you whenever you are using sharp stuff, just in case. However, it's even better to take a first aid kit for any bushcraft activity, and know how to use it.

FIRST AID IS IMPORTANT IN ANY SITUATION, BUT ESPECIALLY WHEN YOU'RE IN A MORE ISOLATED ENVIRONMENT. IF YOU DON'T HAVE A CLUE ABOUT FIRST AID, GET YOURSELF ON A COURSE

Cord – Last, but by no means least, you're going to need cord. Paracord is great to take out with you and will save you lots of hassle when making shelters or traps, or any other activity where string needs to be used. Inexpensive to purchase, paracord is available from online stores and camping shops.

Fire lighting – A cheap disposable lighter, a box of matches, a fire steel or a flamethrower (the latter might be overkill!). However, all will do the job of igniting your fires.

That's it, simple; a knife, saw, cord, first aid kit, appropriate clothes and fire lighting equipment; this is the minimum you will need.

Now, of course you can get as much as you like and there are loads of bushcraft shops out there with all manner of equipment: tarps, sleeping bags, rucksacks, hammocks, axes; the list is endless. However, we would recommend testing stuff and researching carefully, as the most expensive stuff is not always the best.

SAFETY

DON'T SKIP OVER THIS, IT'S IMPORTANT!

So you've got this book – great, it's a good start. You have your kit, you have assembled your tribe and you're off to the woods for a family adventure, excellent!

Make sure you tell someone where you are going. Regardless of whether you're heading out to the middle of Dartmoor or just the local woods, it's wise to let someone know so that if something goes wrong and you become stranded, your phone's dead, the squirrels have nicked your car keys and it starts to bucket it down, someone can raise the alarm and come and get you.

Bushcraft is relatively safe when you are starting out or doing family things. Nothing in this book should lead you to a survival situation where you have to eat insects and drink your own wee to see you through. If you act safely from the start then safety becomes a habit. So when you start your big adventures, which we are sure you will once you catch the bug, your risk will be far lower.

SHARP STUFF

Hominids have been using sharp edges to help make life easier for at least two and a half million years. Knives and other sharps are wonderful tools that have helped shape the development of mankind.

Knives are really important for bushcraft; making things, preparing fire lighting materials, cooking and most other tasks are very difficult without one.

However, sharp things have become scary; knives are associated with 'youths' rather than boy scouts. In the world of bushcraft, we can begin to change the way knives are perceived.

Letting young people learn to use knives to help them explore and enjoy the great outdoors can be a very positive thing. Teach your tribe to use knives safely and responsibly and there is no reason why they shouldn't use sharp edges without you having to worry.

Anyone that uses a knife will cut themselves occasionally: knife injuries help to remind you of the need to be careful with any tool that has a sharp edge.

Very young (six and under) children should only use knives under direct 'contact' supervision, e.g. your hands over their hands when using a blade.

Young children (six to ten) should only use knives under direct supervision.

Children (ten to 14) should only use knives for specific tasks under your direction.

You know your children best; be aware that even the most mature child can sometimes have a lapse of concentration.

Older children (14 and over) are more likely to be able to look after and use their own knives; they should be complimented and rewarded for being responsible and safe knife owners.

There are many videos online that describe the safest way to use sharp tools. Watch them and encourage your tribe to watch them; they contain far better demonstrations of the safest way to use these tools than can be described on paper.

Enter 'bushcraft knife safety video' into your preferred search engine and you'll have lots of guidance.

" Young children should only use knives under direct supervision "

KNIVES

Choosing a knife

There are many, many knives that can be used for bushcraft: penknives, folding knives, locking knives, fixed-blade, full tang, 'Scandi' grind, full grind, convex grind, high carbon steel, stainless steel, 01 steel, D2 steel, the list is endless.

Useful types of knife for the activities in this book:

Penknife/Multi tool

The classic Swiss army knife falls into this category as does any tool that has a knife blade/s accompanied by a number of other devices that fold out of the handle. These knives can be great to stick in your pocket to accompany you on a walk but have some limitations should you rely on them for lots of different tasks.

PENKNIFE

THE BLADES ON THESE TOOLS ARE NOT STRONG ENOUGH FOR MANY TASKS AND MAY BREAK, LEAVING YOU WITH NO KNIFE AT ALL

FOLDING KNIFE

Folding knives

A single-bladed knife that folds out from its handle, traditionally called pocket knives and carried for convenience to help with everyday tasks that call for a sharp blade:

- sharpening pencils
- cutting string
- whittling sticks

LOCKING KNIVES CAN BE A USEFUL 'BACKUP KNIFE' IN THE WOODS

LOCKING KNIFE

Locking knives

A (usually) larger single-bladed knife that folds out from its handle and locks in place with a simple mechanism. Locking knives can be a useful 'backup knife' in the woods and, when used safely, can complete lots of bushcraft jobs well.

Fixed-blades

A blade that is fixed in place, that doesn't fold and that needs a sheath to be carried safely. A 'full tang' fixed-blade knife is a knife that utilises the same length of steel to construct both the blade and the handle, this is the strongest way of making a knife. We think that this makes it **the safest type of knife** as it is less likely to break or fail.

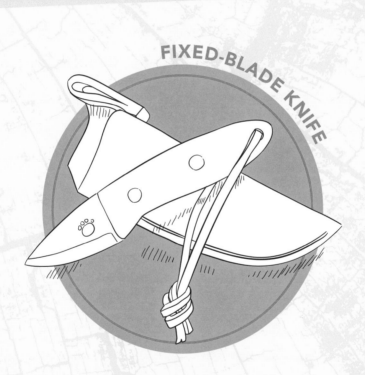

FIXED-BLADE KNIFE

A 'FULL TANG' FIXED-BLADE KNIFE IS LESS LIKELY TO BREAK OR FAIL, AS THE BLADE AND THE HANDLE ARE MADE FROM ONE LENGTH OF STEEL

The most useful knife for bushcraft is a fixed-blade knife made out of steel that you can confidently sharpen and look after.

Size is important. The ideal blade length of a fixed-blade bushcraft knife is about 3 inches and the handle should feel comfortable in your hand.

TIP

A good bushcraft knife can be very inexpensive. Stainless steel will be easier to maintain, but carbon steel can be easier to sharpen.

If you can afford it then a full tang knife will be most reliable and last you the longest.

If you are keen for your children to get involved in bushcraft your tribe ought to get used to handling knives correctly. Giving your child a knife can be a wonderful way to teach them to be safe when using sharp tools while giving them responsibility for caring for, cleaning and sharpening something that belongs to them.

IF YOU FEEL THAT SOME OF YOUR TRIBE ARE A LITTLE YOUNG TO HAVE THEIR OWN KNIFE THEN WHY NOT GIVE THEM ONE AS A GIFT BUT LOOK AFTER IT FOR THEM WHEN THEY ARE NOT USING IT WITH YOUR SUPERVISION?

THINGS TO DO

Make the perfect marshmallow stick

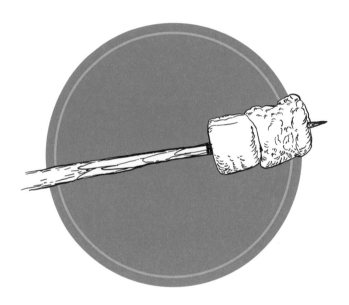

If your tribe are going to enjoy toasting marshmallows to the fullest then they should create their own toasting sticks.

Something at least as long as your forearm and somewhere between a pencil and your little finger in thickness is perfect. The pointy end should be carefully sharpened and the bark removed for a few inches behind the point.

Really young children can safely manufacture a brilliant pointy stick and toast the perfect marshmallow; sit them between your legs, hold their hands in yours and get to work. Make sure they realise what a good job they are doing and how much tastier the finished marshmallow is going to be because they have toasted it.

SHAVINGS, FEATHER STICKS AND FIRE DARTS TO HELP START FIRES

Make shavings

With a little practice it's really, really easy to make shavings that are brilliant for helping to start fires.

Sit your tribe down, elbows on knees, knives in hand and show them how to take slivers of wood from a stick, the thinner the better, but everything can be used.

Make feather sticks

Feather sticks and fire darts are used as tinder to start fires **(see Fire chapter, page 30)**. They are great when natural tinder is a little damp.

Making feather sticks can prove tricky. Once everyone has had lots of practice making shavings then get them to try making a feather stick.

Shave a stick, just like you would to make shavings, but don't finish the cut, so that each shaving is left attached to the stick by a small amount of wood.

Making feather sticks is a great skill to practise and can be perfected over years of fun in woods.

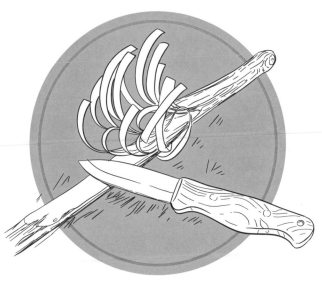

Make a fire dart

Like a feather stick, a fire dart can be used to help light a fire in damp conditions. It's made in a similar way, except instead of shaving only one side of a stick you shave all the way around one end, creating a feather duster-like appearance. The point you leave on the stick when the fire dart breaks off is perfect for starting the next fire dart.

Make a walking stick

Take a stick that seems to be about the right height, weight and thickness for you to use as a walking stick and slowly, carefully strip the bark from it. A coat or two of mineral oil or hazelnut oil on the debarked stick will give you a walking stick that will last ages.

If you can find a straight section of hazel that has a natural fork, twist or burl at one end, then it's very easy to create something beautiful and unique just using a bushcraft knife and a little elbow grease.

AXES

Axes are great tools for splitting wood, carving and other jobs around the camp. We don't recommend that you try to chop through any branch thicker than your wrist with an axe; it'll take ages and can be quite dangerous.

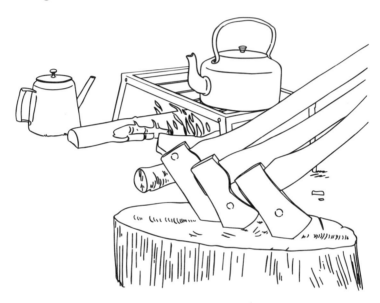

Axes are great at starting carving jobs when you need to remove a lot of wood to start shaping. Hold the axe just behind the head and use its weight to help you as much as possible.

It's much safer to kneel down when using an axe; make sure that the only part of the body that is close to the cutting edge is the hand holding the axe handle (not your knees!).

When using an axe make sure you're aware of your surroundings – don't use an axe if there are people close to you as a flying chunk of wood can leave a big bruise.

Really young children don't have the strength or control to uses axes safely, while older children should only use axes under direct supervision.

SAWS

Folding saws are cheap, lightweight, compact and tough enough to cut through any wood you're likely to need to use while in the woods.

Saws are used to cut firewood and construction materials quickly and cleanly. If you're cutting green wood always try to cut as low as you can and make the cut in the direction that is best for the tree you are cutting. This usually means angling your cut away from the main growth of the tree to allow rain water to run off, away from the tree. If you're cutting firewood that may need to be split, try to make your cuts perpendicular and straight to make the job of splitting with your knife or axe as easy and safe as possible (it's easier to stand an evenly cut log onto a flat surface for safe splitting).

Bow saws are less compact than folding saws, and quality will cost a little more money, but they can be more efficient when handling thicker wood. Never attempt to use a bow saw with two people; you'll end up hurting someone.

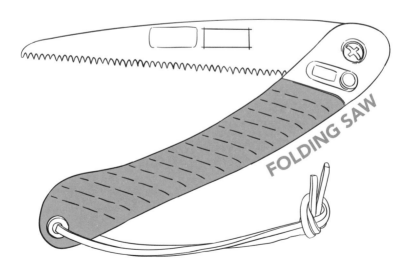

FOLDING SAW

# NOTES

....
....
....
....
....
....
....
....
....
....
....
....
....
....
....
....
....

FIRE

" A fire in the woods on your own is good; a fire with friends and family is excellent "

Before there was TV people sat around the fire.

Fire brings people together; it touches something primeval in us all. Sitting around a fire somewhere wonderful is an experience that should be shared on a regular basis. A fire in the woods on your own is good; a fire with friends and family is excellent.

With a little preparation lighting a fire is simple; to make things really easy start your fire-lighting adventure on a dry, warm day. Once you become a fire-lighting Jedi, you can practise your skills in more challenging conditions.

Later in this chapter you will find loads of different ways to start your fire using friction, sparks, chemicals or the sun.

Whatever method you decide to use the preparation for your fire will usually be the same, you're going to need some fuel to feed the flames and really fine material to start your fire, getting progressively bigger and heavier as the fire builds.

To practise your set-up we recommend starting with a box of matches or a cheap disposable lighter.

SAFETY

Clear the ground as much as possible; there should be no flammable material within a metre of your fire area. Lighting fires on gravel or rock is great as there's is no chance of the fire spreading although you should be extra careful if it's windy. For best results, place two lengths of timber as thick as your wrist parallel with each other and palm width apart in the middle of your cleared area. We normally call these lengths of timber the 'tracks'.

You can also make a base for your fire by laying a bed of sticks really close together in the centre of your fire area. This base will stop damp from rising into your fire and improve your chances of success.

WHAT YOU'LL NEED

TINDER

Tinder is any fine, dry, fibrous material that takes a flame very, very easily. Any of the following work really well:

- dried grass
- newspaper
- cotton wool
- firelighters
- birch bark
- tumble dryer lint

Collect at least two good double handfuls of tinder.

KINDLING

Kindling is dry, thin, light wood that is laid on top of the tinder once it is alight; it needs to be fine enough to catch a flame but thick enough to burn for a while without going out. The ideal kindling is usually the length of your arm from wrist to elbow and is no thicker than your index finger. Ideally you will collect two piles; one that varies in thickness from matchstick to pencil and another that ranges from pencil to index finger size. Your bundles of kindling should be big enough so you can only just hold them with two hands.

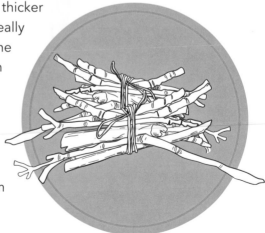

FUEL

To fuel your fire you'll need wood that is dry; anything that is still 'green' or wet just makes things much harder. The ideal fuel is usually as long as your arm from elbow to fingertips. Ideally you will collect two piles; one that varies in thickness from index finger to thumb to help you get the fire going and another that ranges from thumb to wrist to keep the fire going. Collect at least two armfuls of fuel; you don't need to use it all at once but if you need it you've got it.

66 Collecting tinder, kindling and fuel is a great job for the kids, especially if you make a competition out of it 99

LIGHTING YOUR CAMPFIRE

- Once you have everything ready, with neat piles of tinder, kindling and fuel, get everyone sat down so they're on hand to help.

- One person should be in 'charge of the fire'; everyone else needs to be on hand to pass fuel.

- Start by placing a pile of tinder between your two lengths of wrist-thickness timber (your tracks) in the centre of your cleared area.

- Light your tinder using one of the methods detailed later in this chapter. Collecting your tinder into a 'nest' held in both hands around your ember or flame and gently blowing into it increases the flow of oxygen and encourages the flames.

- Gently place a bundle of kindling across your tracks. Blow gently at the very bottom of your small fire to help the fire burn hotter and more evenly.

- Once your kindling is burning well start to gently place your fuel on the fire; start with your smallest little-finger-width sticks and add thicker fuel as your fire gets bigger and is burning hotter. Within a few minutes you will have a fire that is burning well; now you just need to add fuel as your fire needs it.

- You have made FIRE! Just you and your family working as a team to create something awesome. Now sit down, break out the marshmallows and enjoy!

 **Fire lighting can be hard. Don't be put off if it doesn't work for you first time!**

We're going to cover some wonderful ways to create fire but remember the process is always the same: **tinder** (dry and fibrous), **kindling** (thicker than a match stick) and **fuel** (thicker than your index finger). Dry dead wood that snaps cleanly is ideal.

Practise lighting fires with different methods and once you're really happy, try making a cup of tea in the rain.

Do everything together, don't let one person take over (Dad!) and you'll create some fantastic memories as well.

Now you know the process of fire lighting, here are several methods for starting your fire. Some are harder than others so don't be put off if it doesn't work for you first time: keep trying and tweaking things and you will soon get it.

WHEN LIGHTING A FIRE, ALWAYS BE AWARE OF WHAT YOU HAVE AROUND YOU AND ON YOUR PERSON THAT COULD BE FLAMMABLE

FIRE STEEL

Fire steels can be bought cheaply online or in camping shops. They consist of a length of 'ferrous' material and a striker, which is made up from different metals. Scraping these together will give you a shower of sparks. It can take a little practice to use and perfect, but when you get it, it will soon become your most-used fire lighting tool, they even work when they are wet.

Place your fire steel on the tinder and firmly scrape your striker down the steel. Too slow and nothing will happen, too fast and you will just ruin your tinder bundle. Drop sparks into your tinder until it catches light and, hey presto, you've done it.

WIRE WOOL AND A 9V BATTERY

This is really simple and a great one for the kids to try.

Get a good handful of wire wool and tease it apart; you need to create a nice large area for this to work. Once you have spread the fibres of the wire, touch the battery terminals to the wool. This creates a short circuit; lots of energy is forced through a very small amount of material causing it to burn. By blowing on the burn you can increase the heat and cause the whole bundle to combust.

Place your tinder bundle on top of the wool and blow to create a flame. The wool can burn out quickly so you need to be well prepared and speedy with this method.

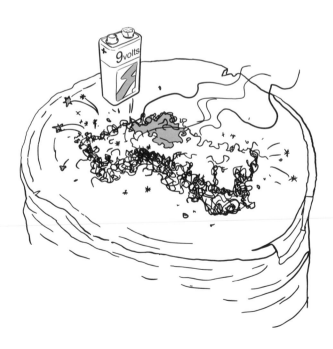

FLINT AND STEEL

One of the more primitive methods of lighting fire is using a bit of flint and a striker made from carbon steel. The idea is to hit the flint with the steel to create a small spark. Now, this may seem easy but it does require a good technique.

Hold the flint in one hand with a nice sharp edge pointing away from you (you're going to hit the sharp edge). Use the steel striker to hit the sharp edge of the flint. You are aiming to just glance the flint edge with the striker. If you get this right you will create a small spark. Bear with it, it does take practice, but it's a great feeling when you can create a spark with every strike.

Once you get your sparks, you need to catch them in your tinder. You could also use a piece of char cloth, a natural-fibre cloth that has been 'burnt' in a sealed container to create cloth 'charcoal'. This can be bought online and is very easy to make yourself out of an old pair of jeans and a tin with a lid in the fire. Another option is a bit of 'King Alfred's Cake'. This is a form of fungus that you'll find stuck to dead or dying ash trees, identifiable as small, hard, black balls that look like the ancient sovereign's burnt cakes.

Once you have caught a spark, gently place it in your tinder and softly blow until you have fire. You're now closer to a caveman than you have ever been! We love creating fire this way, and never tire of it.

SOLAR

This method is easy. The hardest part is getting a good, strong bright sun in the UK.

Take a magnifying glass and allow the sun to shine through it. Focus the sun's rays to a point, aim at the tinder and wait. Stay steady and it will start to char, then smoke and then you will get a flame.

FRICTION

Friction is by far the hardest way to create fire – we could write a chapter on friction fire lighting on its own. Don't get bogged down with the ins and outs, dos and don'ts. Just get stuck in and play; this is meant to be fun after all and not a survival test.

You will need a bow, drill, hearth board, bearing block and an ember pan. You're aiming to spin the drill on the hearth board whilst applying pressure with the bearing block to create heat. This heat will then begin to create smoke and then a sticky black dust will begin to collect on the ember pan. When you have a good amount, stop drilling and get your breath back. Allow the dust to bond and it will start to glow. Place this in your tinder bundle and blow until you create a flame.

Here is a step-by-step pictorial guide to give you the idea of what you need to be doing.

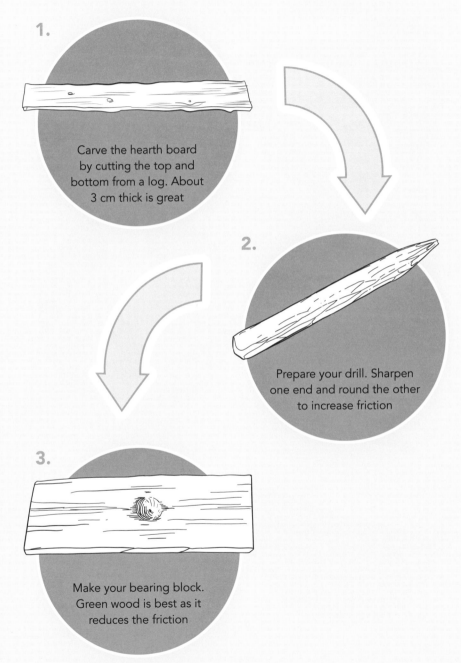

1.

Carve the hearth board by cutting the top and bottom from a log. About 3 cm thick is great

2.

Prepare your drill. Sharpen one end and round the other to increase friction

3.

Make your bearing block. Green wood is best as it reduces the friction

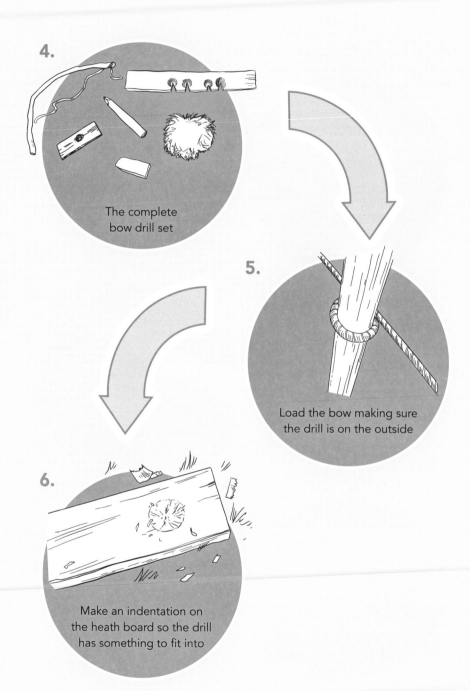

4.

The complete bow drill set

5.

Load the bow making sure the drill is on the outside

6.

Make an indentation on the heath board so the drill has something to fit into

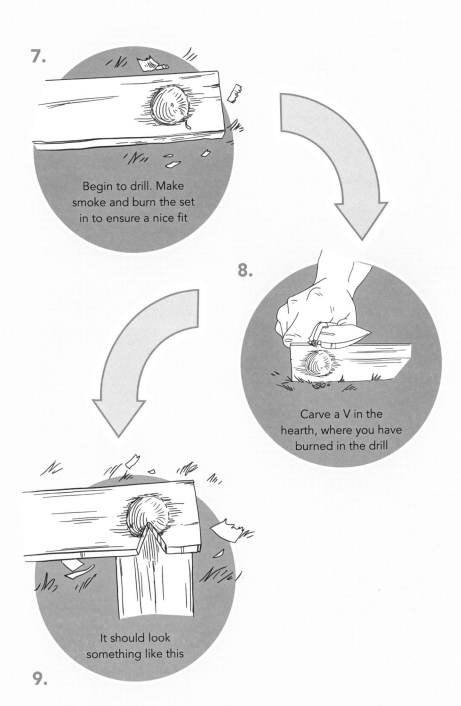

7. Begin to drill. Make smoke and burn the set in to ensure a nice fit

8. Carve a V in the hearth, where you have burned in the drill

9. It should look something like this

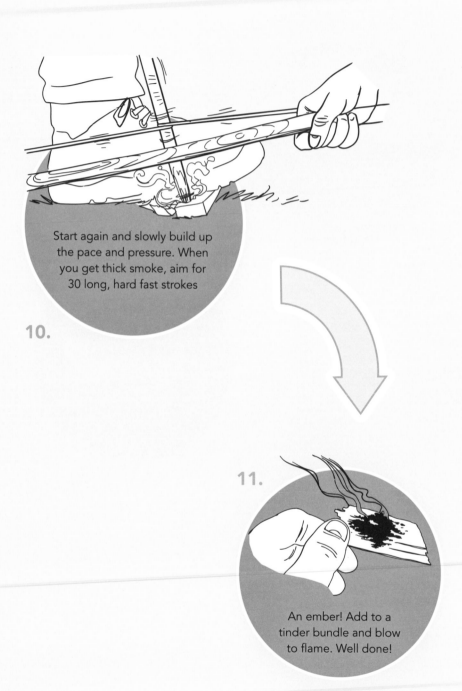

10. Start again and slowly build up the pace and pressure. When you get thick smoke, aim for 30 long, hard fast strokes

11. An ember! Add to a tinder bundle and blow to flame. Well done!

NOTES

....
....
....
....
....
....
....
....
....
....
....
....
....
....
....
....

WATER

> **" You can survive three days with no water and three weeks without food so it's clear where priorities should be "**

Water is essential to life, it's that straightforward.

Whether you are out for a day's walk or a month-long expedition, you need to drink.

It is easy to take water for granted. We are lucky enough to live in a country where we just turn on a tap and have safe, clean drinking water. You only have to become dehydrated for a day to realise how miserable it is: symptoms include a dry mouth, headaches and dizziness. You can survive three days with no water and three weeks without food so it's clear where priorities should be.

Water is heavy, very heavy: one litre of water weighs one kilogram and you are going to need three litres per person per day to keep you well hydrated on your adventures. Mum and Dad won't want to carry all of it by themselves.

You need to be thinking about where your next water top-up is coming from if you are out in the wild for a few days as you cannot feasibly carry several days' worth of water. Care should always be taken about a source of water though. As inviting as the crystal clear stream looks, even the clearest of water can harbour nasties that can make you ill.

But don't worry because it's easy to make water safe to drink, really easy. It is also a task you can do in your back garden and is a fun thing to do with the kids, giving them some fundamental skills to fall back on as they head out to bigger and wilder environments.

Finding and processing water is a key bushcraft skill and it will give everyone a much greater appreciation and respect for water. Firstly we'll discuss ways in which you can find water, and then we'll describe ways in which you can make sure it's safe to drink.

HOW TO FIND AND COLLECT WATER

There are several methods to find water:

- Low ground and the bottom of gullies are a good place to start. Remember water moves downwards so don't start looking on the top of hills!

- Hollows in trees where the branch meets the trunk can act as a natural water collection point.

- Animal tracks are excellent indicators of a water source nearby, especially when you have several different animal tracks on the same trail. Follow the tracks and you stand a very good chance of finding the wet stuff.

What if you can't find any, then what?

If you have no luck finding any water then you're going to have to get creative. It's not as hard as you might think. Have a go at collecting water as a family and try different methods to see who collects the most. Here's how:

IT'S CRUCIAL TO CLEAN COLLECTED WATER BEFORE YOU DRINK IT – YOU'LL FIND OUT HOW LATER IN THIS CHAPTER!

RAINWATER

What you will need

- Tarp
- Bucket

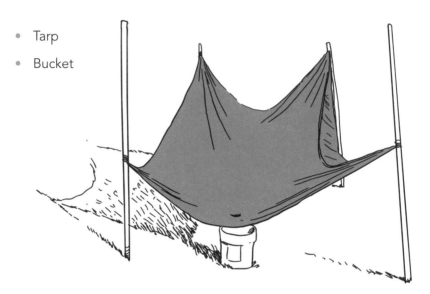

What you should do

Set up a tarp over the bucket (or other large container) so that the water can run off and collect in your bucket. It's a good idea to place a clean tea towel over the container to stop anything falling or crawling in, slugs love a bucket full of water!

Now this method is great if it's raining but it's limiting when it's not, so what then?

COLLECTING THE MORNING DEW

What you will need

- T-shirts

What you should do

This is fun no matter what your age and is a firm family favourite when we go camping.

You need to wake up nice and early. Tie a clean T-shirt to each ankle by knotting the sleeves together. Then walk though some grass, the longer the better. Walk and shuffle along, soaking up all the morning dew.

When your T-shirt is soaking wet, wring it out and see who has managed to collect the most.

Be warned that if you do this on a manicured and sterile campsite you will get some very funny looks from the caravanners, but don't worry about it, life is all about who is having the most fun.

TRANSPIRATION BAGS

What you will need

- Sun
- Clear plastic bag
- Tree

What you should do

You can collect water from trees by placing a clear plastic bag over a branch. The aim is to get as much leaf material in the bag as possible.

As the sun shines on the bag, it heats up and draws the moisture from the plant. The moisture evaporates and forms on the bag as condensation and drips in to the corner of the bag ready for collection.

Be sure to never use any poisonous trees or plants such as rhododendron. If in doubt about which trees or plants are poisonous do not use this method.

Start with trees you know well. Oak, silver birch and beech are good species to try. Experiment with different types of trees and see which ones work the best for you. A handy hint is to make sure the bag is sealed as tightly as possible to minimise the escape of moisture.

SOLAR STILL

What you will need

- Sun
- Spade
- Stone
- Container
- Plastic sheet
- Earth/sand
- Green plants/leaves

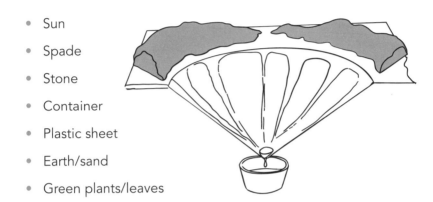

What you should do

This method is good to try, but it would be our last resort as making this is going to cost a lot in sweat and energy. Should you ever need to put this method into practice for real you need to start the process while you still have a good amount of water available for your needs. Hopefully you and your tribe are never going to find yourselves in that situation, but it is still good to have a go to see how it works.

- Start by digging a hole in the ground deep enough to place a bucket or something similar in.
- Now fill the hole with plants, leaves or whatever you can get your hands on that's green. Be careful you're not using poisonous plants.
- Do not cover the container as you need it open to catch the water.

- If you really must do something with your pee now's the time. Pee on the plants; this will add more moisture to the still.

- Cover the hole with a clear plastic sheet and weigh down the edges with stones.

- Cover the edges with earth or sand to form a seal around the sheeting.

- When you're happy, place a stone on the top of the sheet and over the bucket.

As the sun heats up, the hole the plastic acts as a greenhouse and condensation forms on the underside of the sheet. This will move to the lowest point in the sheet and drop into your bucket. Don't expect to get much out of it though; it's one for a baking hot summer's day. Great in the desert, not so much on Dartmoor!

MAKING WATER SAFE TO DRINK

Of course collecting water is all well and good but how do you make it safe to drink?

The fun comes when you start to improvise a water filter

The common contaminants you are going to come across in collected and found water are:

Turbidity – Soil, mud, etc.
Bacterial – Salmonella, E. coli
Parasitic worms
Chemicals
Viruses

Whatever water you collect it is always wise to filter it, be it through a man-made shop-bought filter or an improvised one. Now, it's easy to use a shop-bought filter, so we won't go in to it. The fun comes when you start to improvise a filter.

IMPROVISED FILTER

What you will need

- Sock/bag
- Sand
- Pebbles
- Straw
- Water

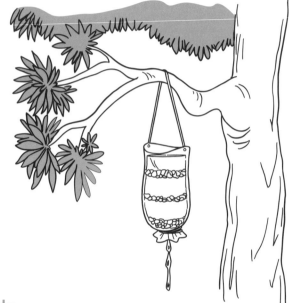

What you should do

Take a sock or bag and fill it with sand, then straw, then small pebbles, then larger pebbles or whatever you can find that will remove all the turbidity. You can then hang it from a tree.

Pour in the dirty water and collect what comes out the other end, hopefully it's cleaner than when it went in!

Once you've tried the above method, have a play, get the kids out and make a filter out of what you can find.

BOILING YOUR WATER

Remember: once you have your filtered water you are going to need to boil it to get rid of the other nasties that reside in it.

It's imperative to boil water for at least four minutes on a rolling boil for it to be safe to drink after filtering. Get it boiling and make sure you have large bubbles on the go, then start the clock. **Remember: BIG BUBBLES, NO TROUBLE!** Do not over boil it as all you are doing is evaporating all your hard work.

If you can successfully collect and clean water in your garden with your kids then you can do it in the woods with no problems whatsoever. Once you have cracked this and are confident with your tribe's skills you will have just unlocked so many more adventures.

Get out there and start experimenting, have fun and enjoy.

"It's imperative to boil water for at least four minutes on a rolling boil for it to be safe to drink after filtering"

NOTES

....

....

....

....

....

....

....

....

....

....

....

....

....

....

....

....

....

NOTES

....
....
....
....
....
....
....
....
....
....
....
....
....
....
....
....
....
....
....

SHELTER

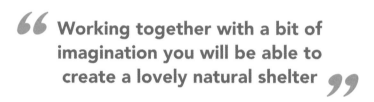

Working together with a bit of imagination you will be able to create a lovely natural shelter

Dens, hides, bases whatever you want to call them, they are a great thing to get the tribe together to build and kids love this activity.

Just take a walk in the woods and you will start to see half-built shelters dotted all over the place, normally in the form of a load of sticks lent up against a tree in a wigwam shape. However, you can do better than that! Working together with a bit of imagination you will be able to create a lovely natural shelter that will keep you warm and dry in the most horrid of weathers.

It's best to establish your skills on a manageable project so start off small in the garden and use everyday things which you have lying around. A great place to start is to build a lean-to type shelter using a broom handle cut in half, an old tarpaulin, rope and some wooden tent pegs which you can make yourself **(see Making Things and Carving chapter, page 176)**. This is a great activity to do together and one that's quick to achieve. Once built, the den is perfect to use as a place to eat lunch, read a book, play cards, etc. As a parent, you could even use your new-found fire-lighting skills to make a fire just on the edge of the den so that your child can shelter within whilst toasting marshmallows on the outside.

Once you've got the hang of den building in the garden, why not progress to the woods?

We want this to be fun so start by building your shelter where there are enough materials around you. It's best to avoid having to drag sticks and logs from miles around, as this is a sure-fire way to put off even the keenest of little explorers. Remember: if it's not fun you're doing it wrong!

SITE SELECTION

Where you choose to build your shelter will depend on the following considerations:

1. **Materials** – As we have already mentioned, choose a place where there are loads of sticks, brash, poles, leaves, ferns and moss to make your life easy.

2. **Comfort** – There is no point in building a five-star, woodland lodge if, as soon as you lay down, you find that the ground is full of hard roots or jagged stones. Top tip – check the floor first!

3. **Wind direction** – Design your shelter so that the back of it is at a 45-degree angle to the ground. This will allow the wind to hit your shelter without causing smoke to be blown in from your fire, if you make one.

4. **Look up** – Be sure to check above to make sure that there are no dead branches or dead standing trees that could fall on you.

5. **Dry** – Check the ground to make sure it is not soaking wet or liable to flood should you get a downpour. Likewise never build any shelter in a dried-up river bed, because if it does rain then you may find yourself being washed away! Sounds dramatic, but it's true.

Happy with your site? Great, let's get building!

The following are a few shelter types that you can have a go at.

TARP SHELTERS

What you will need

- Tarp – They come in loads of different sizes and materials
- Cord – Simple paracord is great

Tents are great but they lock you away from the great outdoors. They also weigh a lot more than a simple tarp. When we teach bushcraft or venture out on our own we always use a tarp, it never gets boring!

All you need is a cheap tarp and some cord. Paracord is ideal, but normal string or bailing twine will work just as well.

With tarp shelters the possibilities are endless; you can set them up however you wish. Here are a few ideas to get you started.

FLAT ROOF

You are going to need to find six trees, spaced out in a rough rectangle to give you somewhere to attach your tarp to.

Fold the tarp in half and attach a line. Normally tarps come with loops or eyelets so use these. Now tie one end to a tree or branch and do the same with the other end. It should now be nice and tight but folded in half.

Stretch out the corners and tie them to branches or tree trunks. You will now have a nice flat roof over your head. With practice you will be able to put a tarp up like this in just a few minutes. Get the kids to put up one each and see who can do it the fastest, a little bit of competition never hurt anyone.

TENT TARP

Much the same as the flat roof, but instead of tying the corners of the tarp up high, tie them low to the ground either at the base of a tree or pegged in to the ground to create an open-ended traditional tent-type shelter. Told you they were simple, that's why we use them!

BEST OF BOTH

This set-up is very adaptable. Set the centre lines as if you are going to make a flat roof but this time tie two corners up high and two close to the floor. This will give you a nice open set-up able to keep you dry from above and offer protection from the wind (remember the 45-degree set-up for the wind).

This is a great one to use if you plan to have a fire.

Test out as many different types of set-ups as you like. Get the kids to set them up and you will be amazed at what they produce. They don't have to be perfect, they just need to work. Once you're happy and confident with your tarp set-ups, try your hand at natural shelters.

NATURAL SHELTERS

Use whatever you can find: logs, sticks, poles, leaves, moss… you get the idea. Mix in a bit of imagination along with your tribe working towards the same goal and you will have something Robin Hood himself would be proud of!

THE LEAN-TO

What you will need

- Ridge pole (straight, long and green branch about forearm thick)
- Two strong forked sticks
- Two trees the right distance apart
- Brash and twigs

What you should do

We love this shelter; it is simple to build and works well with a campfire. It works so well in fact that it is possible to sleep quite comfortably with no sleeping bag in –15°C.

First up you need to find two trees just over the body length of the tallest person. Next you need to find or cut a ridge pole; this should be alive and be able to support your body weight. Once you have this, grab two forked sticks about chest height of the tallest person, these too should be alive.

You now need to place the forked sticks on the **inside** of the trees you have selected. Then place the ridge pole in the forks **behind** the tree trunks. This stops any lateral movement and helps it from falling over. Adjust the angle of the forked sticks to approximately a 45-degree angle. The ridge pole should now sit just below chest height of the tallest person. Now for the test! Cameras at the ready kids, Dad now needs to test the strength of the ridge pole. Hang your whole bodyweight on the centre of the ridge pole and if it does not snap you are good to continue.

Place sticks and branches at the same angle of the forked sticks about every foot or so. They should rest on the ridge pole and be about 6 inches higher than it.

Once you have done this, get branches and brash and lay them across the upright sticks. Your lean-to should now be starting to take shape. Place the brash all over the upright poles and once you have done this, chuck dead leaves or spruce branches over the shelter. Start from the bottom and work your way up.

Check what it looks like from inside and if you can see any sunlight coming through put more leaves on. You are looking for a covering approximately fist to elbow deep to ensure you stay nice and dry if you sleep in it. Go on, you're tempted to now, right?

Keep at it until you're happy and, there you go, your first lean-to shelter is built. Now it's time to get in it, chill out and enjoy your handiwork. If you're short on time or don't fancy making an adult-sized shelter, make a smaller version just for the kids. Whichever size you decide to make, do it together, enjoy, most of all, have fun.

THERMAL 'A' FRAME

What you will need

- Ridge pole (straight, long and green branch about forearm thick)
- Two strong forked sticks
- Brash and twigs

What you should do

This type of shelter is great if you don't have the ability to make a fire. It works by using your own body heat to heat the structure.

You need a ridge pole and the forked sticks, just like the lean-to. However, this time place one end of the ridge pole on the floor. If possible wedge it at the bottom of a tree to stop it sliding away. Put the other end of the ridge pole in the forked sticks and adjust them so the sticks are supporting the pole on its own. Be sure to interlock the forks so that you get the maximum possible support.

Once you have a good stable frame you are then ready to build up the sides. Unlike the lean-to, you'll need to gather different size sticks to build the sides of the shelter but the technique is the same. Once the sides are built use brash and branches to cover the structure. Just like the lean-to dump leaves or spruce branches on the sides and build it up so it is fist to elbow thick.

This is a great shelter to use for animal spotting as it allows you keep warm, stay hidden and camouflaged. Build it, lay a roll mat inside it and hunker down and see what wildlife you can see. Stay quiet and you will be amazed at what you will spot.

WOODEN TEEPEE

What you will need

- Six long straight forked sticks

- Lots of long straight poles

- Brash, leaves and lots of them

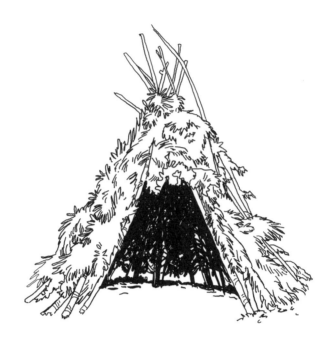

What you should do

This is a shelter which requires lots of long straight poles, six of which need to be forked.

You need to lock the six poles in place to form a triangle type frame and then fill in the sides with the other poles to create a classic teepee or wigwam shape. Try to leave a hole at the very top to act as a chimney.

As previously described in the instructions for building the other shelters in this section, fill in the sides with brash and leaves. Remember to start at the bottom and work up. Keep looking from the inside out to check for sunlight. Using this shelter you will be able to have a small fire inside, so be sure you have left a hole in the top!

This is a fantastic shelter to build as a family. Get everyone working together and the job will be done in no time. Once it's finished get inside and enjoy. Get a small fire going, get some hot chocolate on the go and create some memories.

NOTES

....
....
....
....
....
....
....
....
....
....
....
....
....
....
....
....
....

CORDAGE

❝ You will be amazed at what you can use to make natural cord ❞

Be warned: natural cord making can become highly addictive!

Whatever you need string for in the home you can be sure that you will need it when in the great outdoors.

You will be amazed at what you can use to make natural cord, from nettles, brambles, willow bark, lime bark, tree roots, saplings… the list goes on. Being able to go in to the woods and find what you need to make cord is a fantastic skill to have and is a satisfying and rewarding process in itself. Just think that if your kids know how to do this when on trips and adventures, be it in the back garden or the remotest place in the world, it's one less thing Mum and Dad have to carry.

Being able to make cord from common plants and trees is not only a cool party trick, it is an essential step towards the further construction of many bushcraft tools and implements, from fishing line and bowstrings for hunting, to lashing poles for shelters and a thousand other uses.

NETTLE CORD

There are tons of materials that offer a good range of cordage possibilities, although the preferred plant-based cordage in the UK is probably the nettle. This is partly because nettles are the easiest plant to find and they are readily available for much of the year. They offer great cordage owing to the length of the fibres from which they are formed, which makes them easy to work with. Nettle makes a cord or braid that can be used effectively for most purposes and can even be woven to make a durable, but coarse, fabric – First World War knapsacks were woven from nettle fibre!

THIS IS A GREAT ACTIVITY TO DO AROUND A CAMPFIRE IN THE EVENING TO KEEP THE TRIBE ENTERTAINED

What you will need

- Nettles – the taller the better
- Gloves – or Dad's hand!
- A stick

What you should do

Firstly, you need to avoid the stinging hairs which are found on the leaves and the stem. You don't want the kids to be put off before they have even started, so use gloves. You can rub the hairs off the plant completely while wearing gloves, then tear off the leaves. If you don't have gloves with you then sacrifice a grown-up's hand for this bit. You can then remove the stingers by wilting it over a fire.

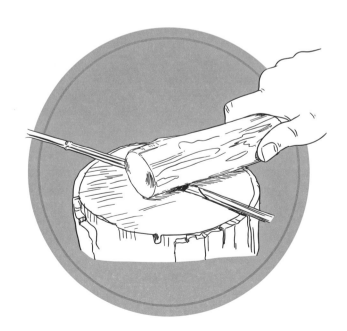

'Wilting' is dead easy. Wave the nettles through the flames of your campfire for a few seconds – this will singe and remove the very fine stinging 'hairs'.

Crush the stem along its length using your fingers or lightly hit them with a stick – don't do it too hard as this can damage the fibres. Remember that you need the outer plant fibres to make nettle cord so protect them as much as possible.

Slide either your fingernail or a knife into the end of the stem and open it up like a book so it can be laid flat.

Remove the inner fibres to leave the outer fibres of the nettle which will serve as your cordage.

The best way to do this is to bend the flat nettle until the inner woody part snaps then push the woody bit up and away from the outer bit. Remember: you need the outer plant fibres so don't chuck that bit away.

Now depending on the thickness of the cord you wish to make, you can use all of the outer fibres in one go or you can thin the stem down by tearing or slicing it lengthways to create a narrower fibre.

More fibres = thicker cord.

Allow your nettle fibre to dry either in the sun or by putting it near a campfire – this is vital, as nettle shrinks when dried and you need that process to happen before you use it. If you're practicing at home then use the radiators to dry it out.

It will only take ten minutes or so to dry near a fire. If the nettle fibres seem brittle then you may need to soak them a little bit to make them more pliable.

Now let's get this cord made!

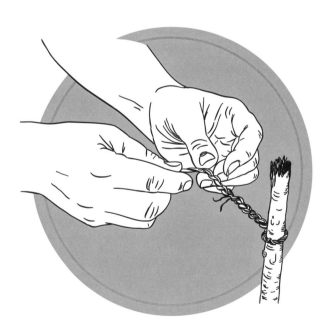

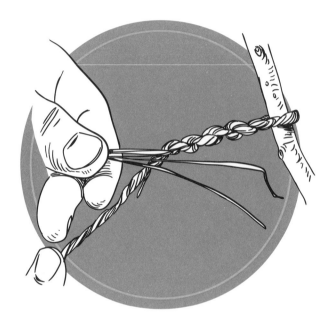

We are going to start by folding one strand of the nettle so that you have one bit longer than the other by about four inches. This is important because when we need to add more nettle in to make longer cord, the joins need to be staggered to provide strength.

Now you need to twist both bits of nettle using your thumb and forefinger in opposite directions until the fibres kink naturally. Keep twisting the fibres in the same direction and the nettle will begin to twist around itself forming your cord. Keep this process up until you begin to run out of fibre on one side.

If you find you are struggling with this, practise on a bit of string or paracord as this will be a bit simpler to start with.

Great! Addicted yet?

To join a new bit of nettle fibre into your cord you are going to want to select a length of fibre roughly the same thickness as the one you started with. Getting the same thickness will allow your cord to be uniform all the way though. No one likes lumpy cord.

Once you have chosen a suitable bit you are going to need to lay the new piece on the shortest part on your cord and twist them together.

Once they are twisted continue the process until you need to add a new join. This is why we had a short and a long bit to start with. Carry on until you have the length of cord you require and finish it off with a basic knot.

You can give your cord extra strength by making another length and twisting these together or you can fold the cord again with a long and short bit and double up the cord. This will provide you with a very strong cord but it will be half the length you previously made.

The possibilities are endless, but the ultimate goal would be to make enough cord for the bow drill set and use that to create fire by friction. For that you're going to need nettles and lots of them!

OTHER CORDS

BRAMBLE

Once you get the hang of the process you can move on to different materials. Bramble is one of our favourites, not only does it make a strong cord but looks very nice at the end as well.

The process is the same as nettle but the preparation is slightly different. You need to remove all the thorns using the back of a knife or a stick and then open it up, just like the nettle. Remove the woody inner as before and keep the outer bit. This stage is a little different to the nettle in that you now need to remove all the green outer skin. Use your thumbnail to scrape it all off and you will be left with a slightly clear yellowish fibre. All you need to do now is twist it just like nettle.

Have a go at joining nettle with bramble and see what happens.

WILLOW

Willow is another great natural material to use for cord. You need to get a willow branch about arm's length and with as few small shoots coming off it as possible. Once you have this you are going to need to very gently scrape off the outer green bark – the back of a folding saw is the perfect tool for the job. Once you have it all off, take a knife and slice down the length of the stick. You can now peel the inner bark off the stick and use that in the same way as nettle to twist in to cord.

SPRUCE ROOTS

The hardest bit in using roots is digging them up. You are going to need to find a suitable spruce tree and then get yourself a strong, sturdy stick. Kneel down and scrape a line in the earth about a metre from the trunk. Keep scraping until you hit roots. They are only just under the ground by about 2–3 cm. Once you have found a good root you are going to need to follow it and try to remove it in one long piece.

TIP Removing single roots won't cause long-term damage, but make sure you don't take a lot of roots from the same tree.

If you have a child that loves getting dirty then this is the job for them!

Once you have your root scrape off the outer bit and, as easy as that, you have cord. You can, if you wish, split this down and twist it to make it more flexible.

Making cord is a great way to while away the hours when camping or when you're out and about on your adventures. You don't have to wait until you go camping though; get out on a walk, try to collect all the natural materials you need and bring them home. Stick the kettle on, get out the chocolate biscuits, turn the TV off and get twisting.

See who can make the finest cord, who can make the strongest or who can make the longest.

Here is a challenge for your tribe. As a team, make some fine cord out of whatever you like best (hint, hint… bramble). Make it as fine as you can and as long as you have the stamina for – about 10 metres would be great. Attach a hook and see if you can catch a fish with it. Yes it can be done!

To really get the creative juices flowing, each make a friendship bracelet and use food colouring to dye them and then swap with each other.

Friendship bracelets are really simple; make a length of cord from dyed, plaited or nicely twisted cord and tie around your friend's wrist.

To make fishing line you'll need a long, fine length of cord (bramble cord is brilliant). When you think you have enough, tie a hook to one end and wrap the other around a stick.

Simple pot hangers can be made with a branch fork and length of cord.

Lengths of natural cord can be used through zippers, as lanyards for knives or fire steels.

You can also use natural cord for anything else you might need a length of string for.

It does not matter what you do, but do it together. Get outside and try different plants and see what works, you will be surprised.

Happy twisting!

❝ Making cord is a great way to while away the hours when camping or when you're out and about on your adventures ❞

 # NOTES

....
....
....
....
....
....
....
....
....
....
....
....
....
....
....
....

NOTES

FORAGING

> ❝ **Foraging is one of the best family activities there is** ❞

Whoever said there is no such thing as a free meal clearly had never been foraging. You would be amazed at what is available to you just on your doorstep. If you have a garden, there could be wild plants that you can eat very close to home.

Foraging is one of the best family activities there is, be it a planned day hunting for wild garlic or picking blackberries on a dog walk; it is deeply rewarding and, better yet, gets the kids excited about good fresh food, and that's always a good thing.

BY LAW YOU ARE ABLE TO FORAGE FOR THE FOUR F'S: FRUIT, FLOWERS, FOLIAGE AND FUNGI. YOU CAN DO THIS ANYWHERE AS LONG AS YOU HAVE THE RIGHT OR PERMISSION TO BE ON THE LAND

THE GOLDEN RULES OF FORAGING

There are six golden rules when it comes to foraging, these are:

1. IDENTIFICATION

If you're not 100 per cent sure what that plant or berry is, do not put it in your mouth! There are plants that can make you very ill, if not kill you, so if in doubt leave it out. The illustrations in this chapter are intended as a guide only.

2. MEDICATION

If you are on any prescription medication beware that some wild plants may have an effect on what the doctor has prescribed. It may increase the effect of the medication or stop it altogether. Again, if in doubt leave it out.

3. ALLERGIES

Just like food from the supermarket you may be allergic to some wild foods. How do you know if you have not tried it before? If you are trying something for the first time don't do it on your own – make sure someone is with you and keep a bit back so, should you have a reaction, you can show the doctor what you've ingested.

If you have any doubts, for any reason, about eating something foraged, then don't!

4. MINORS

Small children have less of a tolerance to wild plants than adults, so as a portion guide each person should only eat what they can fit in the palm of their hand.

5. HOW MUCH TO EAT

As you gain experience and become confident using foraged food you will learn what can be used in abundance and what should be used for flavour and garnish. Just because there's loads of something doesn't mean you can or need to use it all.

6. SAFE SOURCING

Be careful where you pick your wild food from. Do not collect it from busy roadsides because of the toxins the plant may absorb – you also run the risk of being hit by a car.

The sides of farmer's fields are also to be treated with care because of the pesticides that are used. Likewise, avoid collecting from below dog-head-height in areas where there is a lot of dog walking traffic, for obvious reasons!

Now, we have not told you all this to scare you and put you off but it would be irresponsible of us not to give you the information you need to keep you and your family safe.

Now let's get to the yummy stuff. What can you go out to find?

THINGS TO FORAGE

NETTLES – *URTICA DIOICA*

Nettles are a good place to start your foraging as they are easily identified. They have jagged leaves which grow in pairs. Nettles range from 55 cm to 2 metres in height. The plant likes rich soil and can be found on waste ground, along beaten tracks and in fact almost everywhere.

Pick the young top leaves of nettles to ensure you get the best of the plant. Older larger leaves will be tough and unpleasant.

You can use the nettle as a leafy green substitute, provided the sting has been removed. Do this by blanching or boiling the nettle so the formic acid that stings you is broken down. We like to use nettle to add to curries and stews and it makes a great alternative for spinach.

Fancy a wild brew? Then grab a handful of nettles and steep in boiling water, allowing to stand for a few minutes. Remove the nettles and enjoy! It's great with a dash of honey and rich in vitamin C.

DANDELION – *TARAXACUM*

Dandelions are another easy-to-find plant. They have a yellow flower and hollow stem when broken. The leaves have large points down the side that resemble lions' teeth which is where the name comes from – it is taken from the French *Dent de lion* meaning lion's tooth.

The leaves are 5 to 25 cm long and the stem grows to around 10 cm. When the plant grows to seed the flower will be a light fluffy downy sphere that can be blown off with ease.

It is traditionally used as a tonic for the liver and as a diuretic. All parts of the plant can be eaten (apart from the fluffy seed heads, we don't recommend eating these). The yellow flowers can be turned into wine or dipped in batter and fried to make fritters, or you can simply add the flowers to a salad. The green leaves should be picked from new plants while they are still small. They can be eaten raw or steamed. The larger older leaves will need to be boiled and are better in stews.

WOOD SORREL – *OXALIS ACETOSELLA*

This tangy little plant is a great wild edible. Resembling a large three-leafed clover, the wood sorrel has heart-shaped flowers that taste like apple peel and is a superb herb to accompany trout. Be warned though that eating wood sorrel in excess can cause diarrhoea. It contains high amounts of oxalic acid and should be avoided by people with kidney problems and arthritis. Do not be put off by this – just remember the golden rules and portion sizes.

ELDERFLOWER – *SAMBUCUS NIGRA*

Elderflower grow in umbels – clusters of small flowers on the elder tree, the bark of which is gnarled and rough to look at. The leaves are serrated at the edge, with each leaf bearing five to seven leaflets. Do not mistake it for other umbels found on single plants, such as fool's parsley and hemlock, which you will see at the side of country roads or in hedgerows. Hemlock is extremely poisonous and can kill.

The flowers on elder can be turned in to elderflower cordial and when the flowers turn to berries it makes a fantastic wine. Making the cordial is a wonderfully simple family activity as everyone can get involved. Pour 3 pints of boiling water over 900 g of caster sugar in a large bowl, stir well and then leave to cool. Next add 50 g of citric acid and add two to three sliced lemons. Now take 30–40 flower heads (pre-shaken to remove any insects) and add them to the liquid, then stir. Keep in the fridge for at least 24 hours (or up to a week, stirring daily). Then strain through a jelly net or muslin cloth into a clean container. You can also dip the flowers in batter and make elderflower fritters, which are very tasty.

BLACKBERRIES – *RUBUS FRUTICOSUS*

We all know what blackberries look like, don't we? Good – that's a relief! What you might not have known though is that the young leaves make a great blackberry leaf tea. Simply infuse a handful of the leaves in boiling water. This is also great if you have an upset stomach as it stops the runs, should you get caught out on your new family adventures.

PLANTAIN – *PLANTAGO MAJOR*

This is your wild first aid kit; as well as being edible, this plant has anti-inflammatory and anti-histaminic properties. Forget dock leaves for getting rid of nettle stings, this is the go-to plant. Insect bite? Wasp sting? Ha! It laughs in the face of them!

All you need to do is grab a handful, mush it up and extract the juice, then rub it on the affected area. It's that simple.

RAMSONS – *ALLIUM URSINUM*

Ramsons (also known as wild garlic) grow in deciduous woodland, and tend to flower in the spring just before the trees start to show leaves.

The plant has oval green narrow leaves that grow from the base of the flower stems that bear white bell-like flowers. When disturbed, the plant smells very strongly of garlic. Beware that it is possible to get this plant mixed up with lily of the valley due to the similar leaves and flowers. This is a highly poisonous plant that does not smell of garlic, instead it has a sweet and heady scent.

You can use ramsons in salads or soups. They can also be used instead of basil to create pesto – just be sure you won't be kissing anyone after.

Ramsons have been used in the past to feed cows so that the milk tastes slightly garlicky. This milk is then made in to butter. It's not for your cornflakes!

So there you have it, seven common, easy to identify edible plants. Once you can identify these with ease, then you can move on. Just remember the golden rules and you and your tribe will have lots of fun. Take a guidebook out with you and see how many plants you can identify from it.

When you're exploring the local countryside get your tribe to try to identify as many plants as possible. If there's something that no one can name take a leaf or flower home to help you work out what it is.

MUSHROOMS

Now you might be thinking what about mushrooms? Well, you can eat wild mushrooms, but this is not a field guide for foraging and mushrooms are a whole different ball game. You only get that wrong once. We would recommend going on a dedicated mushroom foraging course and seeking professional help if you want to start collecting fungi.

Now get out there and start eating for free, it's the way forward.

Ink cap – would you eat this?!
Answer: NO! It is very poisonous.

NOTES

HUNTING TOOLS

❝ Hunting with appropriate and legal equipment for food/ pest species is a great skill ❞

The important stuff...

Nothing that can be considered a weapon or that can cause injury or harm should EVER be picked up, aimed or used when there is ANY chance that it could hurt someone.

You should never pick up, aim or use anything which could be considered a weapon or hunting tool when there is any chance that you could hurt an animal unless you are trying to legally and humanely kill that animal for food or pest control.

We think that hunting with appropriate and legal equipment for food/pest species is a great skill to learn but some of the implements described in this chapter are ancient technology and should be treated as such. Use accurate and humane tools to kill; to use anything else is unnecessary, cruel and usually illegal.

Targets

Targets that won't break your weapons are essential; they can be bought or made very cheaply. Targets can be as simple as a carrier bag filled with leaf litter or hay.

Make sure that all your targets are positioned in such a way that you can clearly see what is behind them, you need to make sure that anything you aim at a target will NOT hurt anyone EVER.

THROWING DART

Throwing darts must only be thrown at targets when it is safe to do so.

The best simple throwing darts are made from hazel or ash poles 3 to 4 feet long and about as thick as your index finger or thumb. Throwing darts should be pointed at one end and have flights or fletchings at the other to stabilise the dart in flight. You can use cord, gaffer tape, big feathers or anything similar to make the fletchings, and use glue or cord to attach them to the spear.

BECKET (CORD DART THROWER)

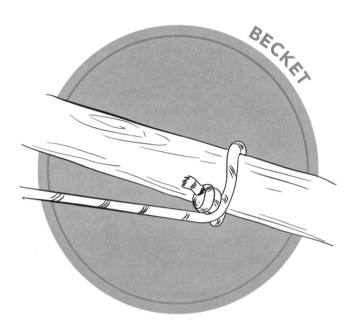

The becket is brilliant fun and is very, very simple. The becket itself is a length of strong cord with a knot in the end. The cord is wrapped once or more around the dart then 'hooked' over the knot and kept tight while holding the spear ready to throw it. When thrown, the cord adds extra leverage and a spin to the spear so you can throw it with more power and accuracy.

❝ **The becket is brilliant fun and is very, very simple** ❞

ATLATL (SOLID SPEAR THROWER)

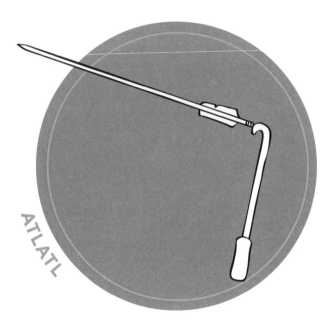

The atlatl or spear thrower is real 'ancient technology' that predates the bow and arrow. It's a simple device that gives your throwing arm a little extra length and leverage, allowing you to throw a spear or dart further and, with a little practice, more accurately.

At its simplest the atlatl is a stick about as long as your forearm from fingertip to elbow with a hooked point or spike at one end.

Spears or darts to be used with the atlatl have simple flights or fletchings and an indentation in the butt (the back) of the spear (i.e. not the pointy end).

The spear is held with the atlatl point resting in the indentation; the throwing hand holds the atlatl and the spear.

When thrown the atlatl extends your arm providing lots of extra power and leverage allowing you to throw the spear a very long way.

To make a very effective and simple atlatl choose a longish branch that has a natural fork. Cut a length as long as you need (as long as your arm from fingertip to shoulder and with an inch or two long spike works really well) on the main growth of the branch above the fork, then trim off the excess from your fork and the branch and shape your point until you have a tool that works for you.

FISHING SPEAR

Spears and spear guns are illegal to use in UK 'inland' waters; you can't use a fishing spear in freshwater like lakes and rivers. It's really fun to use a fishing spear on shallow beaches or other tidal water.

Fishing spears are made to try to stop fish sliding off the point (or points) of your spear once you've skewered it. Fishing spears are usually longer than spears made for throwing as they are usually thrust or jabbed into the fish.

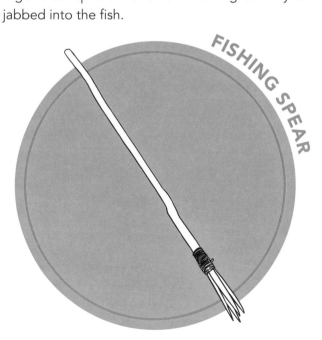

There are a number of different designs that can be made; the easiest is the four-pronged fishing spear.

Four-pronged fishing spear

- Take a long pole cut from some hazel (ideally) and lash some cord tight around the shaft about 30 cm from the end that looks like it will split most easily (the end with the fewest knots). A good length of hazel is perfect for this.

- Split the end of the spear and use two small lengths of wood to hold your split sections open. Lash a good length of cord below your split to hold everything in place.

- Carefully split the lashed end of the pole as far as the cord (the cord is in place to stop the wood continuing to split).

- Use two small lengths of wood (thin rounds or pieces split from a thicker section are fine) to push down the slits and hold the four sections open. The small lengths will form a cross at the base of the splits.

- Lash more cord around the small lengths to hold them in place and make the spear secure.

- The splayed points are better at stopping a fish sliding off your spear and also give you more chance of hitting your target.

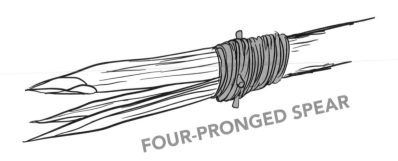

FOUR-PRONGED SPEAR

BOW AND ARROW

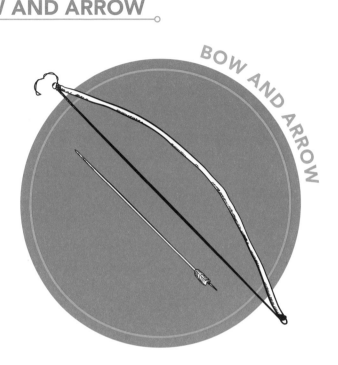

Everyone should have a go at making and shooting their own bow and arrow at least once – it's loads of fun. A really simple (but not very powerful) bow and arrow can be made by using a bendy stick and some good quality cord; green hazel or sycamore work nicely, as does paracord or braided fishing line.

Simple bow

- Grab a helper, if there is one available, and tie the string securely to one end of the stick.

- Bend the stick and tie the cord to the other end so the bow is bent and the cord is under tension. It can help to cut notches in each end of your bow to help the string sit in place nicely.

- If you want to get really fancy you can wrap, or whip, some cord around the middle of your bow to make a handle.

- To pull back or 'draw' your bow hold it with your weakest hand and draw the string back with your strong hand. You can either hold the arrow onto the bow or cut your notches tight enough that your arrows hold themselves in place.

- You can make a more powerful bow by using longer lengths of wood. If you can find a piece of standing, seasoned hazel that bends without cracking you can make a fairly powerful bow without having to use any tools at all.

Once you've had a bit of practice start shaping and perfecting your bows – there's lots of information online to help you do this. We often have a stash of hazel and ash poles stored in the garage seasoning for next year's bows. If you use the best materials and take lots of care making your bow you may end up with something fantastic that will last for years.

> DON'T STORE YOUR BOW WITH THE STRING UNDER TENSION OR THE WOOD WILL 'FOLLOW THE STRING' AND BECOME MISSHAPEN. RUB IT DOWN WITH SOME OIL EVERY NOW AND AGAIN AND IT'LL LAST FOR MANY, MANY COMPETITIONS

To make advanced 'arrows' it helps to have a knife, some feathers, some cord and some glue.

We think that wing feathers from Canadian geese make great fletchings and they can often be found in parks or next to rivers. Pheasant or duck also work well; make sure you save some long feathers next time you're making dinner.

" Archery competitions are excellent fun "

Arrows

- Sharpen one end of your straight stick to make the business end of your arrow and cut a notch in the other end that fits the string of your bow tightly.

- Use feathers to make your fletchings, you'll first have to split them in half along the quill (the middle bit of the feather). Cut off the thick section of a long feather with scissors or your knife, then split the feather in two.

- If your feather is long enough you might be able to get two or three fletchings from each side of the feather. Remember; you'll need some 'spare' length to attach them to your arrow.

- If you're using wing feathers you'll notice that each fletching has a natural curl, make sure that you only use feathers that curl the same way so that your arrows spin in flight and are extra accurate.

- Use glue and thin cord (dental floss works nicely) to attach your fletchings evenly around the notched end of your shaft. Try using two or three on each arrow.

- Experiment with different length fletchings from different birds until you've found what works best for you.

There are lots of ways to make bows so that they are powerful and accurate; experiment, see what you prefer and teach your friends.

CATAPULT

As long you have permission from the landowner to shoot over land, then hunting 'pest species' with a catapult is perfectly legal; you'll need to be absolutely sure that you know, understand and abide by the law and game legislation (www.gov.uk/hunting/overview).

Made famous by classic comics like *The Beano*, a catapult should be owned by anyone who spends time outdoors.

Catapults are easy to make and lots of fun to use, provided they are used responsibly. All you need is a robust forked stick, some decent elastic and some targets. Tin cans are great to start with but once everyone has had a chance to practise, paper targets may well be needed for accurate scoring. Homemade catapults can be very accurate.

Catapults are great for taking on woodland walks or day trips to the woods in the hope of killing your dinner; they are compact enough to carry in a pocket with some ready ammunition and are more than up to the task of taking down rabbits, pigeons or squirrels.

If you are hunting anything for food you must be very confident that you can achieve a quick, clean, humane kill with the weapon you are using.

Catapults don't have a very large effective range; for hunting purposes they should only really be used at a maximum range of about 15 metres. Catapults use heavy ammunition which packs a lot of punch. At close ranges and used by someone that has practised enough to know they are accurate a catapult is an effective and humane weapon for taking small game and pest species.

Catapults are perfect as a first project for young people to make in the woods. Children can, with supervision and guidance, create something that will last them for ages.

CREATING A CATAPULT

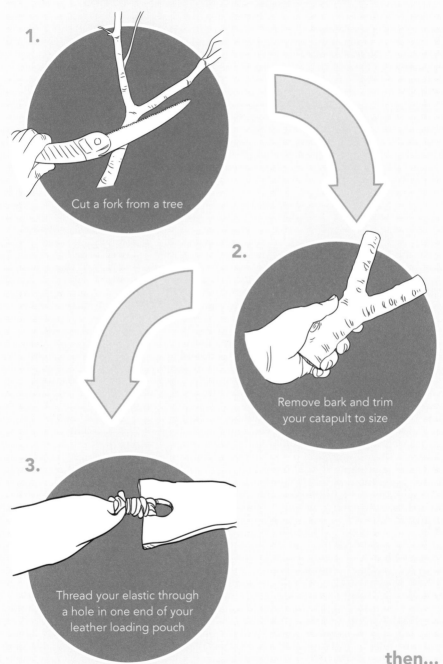

1. Cut a fork from a tree

2. Remove bark and trim your catapult to size

3. Thread your elastic through a hole in one end of your leather loading pouch

then...

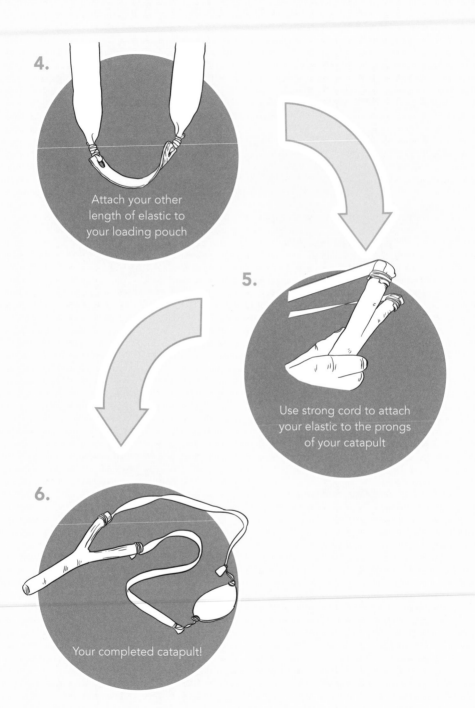

4. Attach your other length of elastic to your loading pouch

5. Use strong cord to attach your elastic to the prongs of your catapult

6. Your completed catapult!

Use small stones, marbles or ball bearings for your ammunition, which is placed in the leather strip before the catapult is pulled back. Try to get used to pulling the elastic back to the same point every time, we find it best to hold the catapult in your weak hand with a straight arm then pull the leather pouch back with your strong hand until it's next to your mouth and the point of your thumb is just touching the corner of your mouth.

If you get used to pulling your catapult back the same distance every time you use it you will become more accurate much quicker.

Be careful with your catapult; they can really hurt people. Make sure that there is absolutely no one 'down range' when you intend to take a shot.

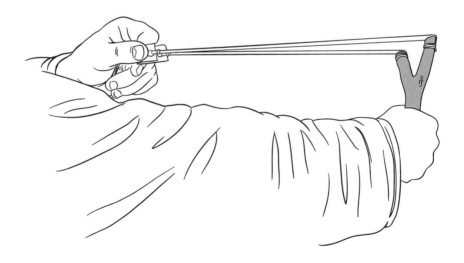

NOTES

PREPARING GAME AND SEAFOOD FOR THE POT

❝ Preparing animals for food and using as much of them as we can will give you and your tribe a better understanding of where meat comes from ❞

In the UK, despite the gradual increase in awareness of animal welfare, organic production and alternative diets, we have lost touch with and lost respect for the animals and processes by which we obtain our meat.

Preparing animals for food and using as much of them as we can, from nose to tail or beak to feather, is a wonderful skill to learn that will give you and your tribe a better understanding of where meat comes from. In this section our aim is to introduce you to the methods of preparing meat from source.

Some people have emotional attachments to some pest species, probably due to their sometimes being kept as pets, or their ubiquitous appearance as cute characters in children's books and cartoons. We think that learning how to prepare animals for the pot is really important; some people (perhaps your tribe) may start off thinking a little differently.

TRY NOT TO PUT PRESSURE ON ANYONE TO GET THEIR HANDS DIRTY OR EVEN WATCH IF THEY DON'T FEEL COMFORTABLE WHILE GAME IS BEING PREPARED

GAME BIRDS

Game birds are great to prepare outside; plucking is far less of a problem when you don't have to worry too much where the feathers are going. The birds listed below are readily available depending on the season. Once you've found a supplier you can ask them to let you know when they have different birds in stock.

This bushcraft skill can really make a difference to the cost of meat to feed a household, especially when certain birds are seasonally available.

Plucking – The trick to plucking is to be firm but gentle, grip the feathers a few at a time and pull them firmly away from the direction of growth. Don't stand downwind of the bird you are plucking or you will end up covered in feathers.

Skinning – Rabbits and squirrels will need to be skinned before cooking them, a sharp knife is really useful; be firm but gentle and use your knife as little as possible. There's lots of videos online that show you great ways to skin small game, try a few techniques and see what works for you.

Gutting – Only use your knife to make a small incision at the base of the breastbone and then use your fingers to open the bird up and scoop out the giblets. We think it's best to do this after you have finished plucking.

We strongly recommend starting with smaller birds first; they are generally easier to work with and young people find gutting them a little less intimidating.

Good birds to start off with are:

Pigeon

Cheap and readily available from game dealers, good butchers, pest controllers or farmers. A quick and simple way to enjoy this bird is to fry the seasoned breasts with bacon then slice and serve on toast or bread.

PIGEON

Partridge

Cheap and readily available from game dealers and good butchers, Partridges are beautiful birds with lovely feathers. Pot roast the whole bird over a fire in wine or stock and lots of root vegetables.

PARTRIDGE

PARTRIDGES ARE ONE OF THE LESS 'GAMEY' TASTING GAME BIRDS, AND HAVE A SUBTLE FLAVOUR

Duck

Wild ducks are smaller than farmed birds but even tastier; pluck the breasts and remove them with the skin still attached. Fry skin-side down first, then flip and fry for a few more minutes. Leave to rest for a few minutes then carve and serve.

DUCK

BECAUSE OF THE HIGH FAT CONTENT, THE FRIED SKIN ON A DUCK, WHEN COOKED WELL, WILL BE CRISPY AND DELICIOUS

PHEASANT FEATHERS MAKE GREAT
FLETCHINGS FOR SPEARS AND ARROWS

PHEASANT

Pheasant

A bird evocative of the British autumn and winter. The cock birds have beautiful feathers which children often love to keep (they're also great for fletching spears and arrows). Pluck and pot roast, or remove the breasts and use for a game stew (like cooking partridge).

PIGEONS AND DOVES ARE PART OF THE FAMILY OF BIRDS CALLED COLUMBIDAE. GENERALLY LARGER SPECIES ARE CALLED PIGEONS AND SMALLER ONES ARE CALLED DOVES

DOVE

Dove

Doves can be treated in the same way as pigeon and taste very similar. Remove the breasts and cook them as you would pigeon.

SMALL GAME

There are many species of wild game in the UK, some of which are considered to be pests and can be seen in abundance (such as rabbits), whilst some are beautiful and a little more elusive (such as hares).

Hare

A species native to the UK that is a little rarer and more expensive than rabbit. Hares can also be harder to catch as they are the fastest mammal in the UK. Cook like rabbit but watch those portions – hare can get BIG.

HARE

RABBIT

Rabbit

Officially a pest species that was introduced to the UK a thousand years ago by the Normans and which bred, well, like rabbits. They can be bought cheaply from game dealers all year round and will probably be gutted prior to purchase (although you can probably ask for a few fresh bunnies to be left intact). Before you can enjoy them they need to be skinned. Skin the rabbit and joint into six portions, and then slow cook in a stew over the fire; rabbit works wonderfully with Mediterranean flavours. Try cooking it in tomatoes, chorizo, wine or stock and herbs – chop everything into your pan, cover with the wine or stock and cook gently for as long as possible.

Grey squirrel

An invasive pest species that is doing its best to decimate the UK's native population of red squirrels, grey squirrel is great for dinner. With a milder taste than rabbit, it can be cooked in exactly the same way or it can be steamed in a foil parcel (with a bit of wine, stock, or citrus fruits) above the fire. Squirrel can be quite hard to get hold of due to a lack of demand; if you get the opportunity to try some then do so.

SQUIRREL

RED SQUIRRELS ARE RARE, WONDERFUL AND A PROTECTED SPECIES. IT IS AGAINST THE LAW TO HARM THEM OR DAMAGE THEIR HABITAT

DEER

Deer are considered pests by many people; they have no natural predators and current populations are unsustainable in most parts of the UK. Deer must be culled to reduce numbers; this is done by shooting them in a managed way. If deer were not shot to reduce numbers they would cause even more damage to crops and woodland, deer populations would become diseased and malnourished, and biodiversity would become threatened in many habitats.

Venison is a wonderful meat choice. Completely free-range and grass fed, it is similar in texture to beef. Venison is usually very lean meat which means it's really good for you. It's also very easy to cook, and can be very cheap to buy. It has more protein than any other red meat as well as loads of iron and B vitamins.

Venison that has been gutted and butchered well will not be tough and should never taste overly gamey. The autumn and early winter is the best time to find and buy venison as it's readily available in butcher's shops. The meat is brilliant after the deer have spent a summer feeding and getting in shape for the rut (the mating season).

TIP

Steaks and quality roasts should be cooked hot and fast, while stewing meat and pot roasts should be cooked low and slow.

Where to get venison/deer from

- The butchers – not always available, usually pre-prepared, expensive
- Game dealers – usually pre-prepared, expensive
- Stalkers (people who shoot deer) – can take a little initial effort to find, usually will only sell whole or half animals, can be very cheap.

What to do with venison

There are many ways to enjoy venison. Here are some of our favourites:

- Get some steaks and cook them over a red hot open fire.
- Get some stewing meat and slow cook it with root veg and wine or stock over a fire.

* Get the whole family together for a special occasion, buy a whole deer carcass with the skin on and skin, butcher and prepare the entire animal. It's not hard to do and is a brilliant activity that brings people together and can finish with a huge, delicious meal.

FISH AND SEAFOOD

There's loads that can be done over a fire with all sorts of creatures that live in the water. It would take several books to describe them all so we're going to suggest some of the most fun and the tastiest to get you started.

SHELLFISH

If you're lucky enough to find mussels, cockles or clams when you are foraging on the shore then cooking them over a fire on or near the beach is magical. They can be steamed in a little salt water in a pan over the fire, baked by covering with embers in a depression in the sand or added whole to stews or soups.

The only tools you need to help to collect shellfish are a bucket and a keen eye, though a trowel, a small rake and some salt can help.

The best time to collect shellfish is at big or 'spring' low tides when lots of rocks and sand are uncovered. Spring tides happen twice every month and, rather confusingly, have nothing to do with the season.

A general rule is that the closer you are to the absolute lowest water mark, the bigger, fatter and tastier the shellfish will be.

Be really careful when collecting shellfish; make sure that you have all the local knowledge you need to stay safe and happy. Only collect shellfish that are tightly closed shut from very clean water and beaches. Dirty water can mean the shellfish harbour lots of bugs, bacteria and other nasties. If in doubt, avoid.

Mussels

Can be found attached to rocks that get covered by the tide.

MUSSEL

Cockles and clams

Can be found in sand that is uncovered by the tide; look for shells that are still upright, so you can see both sides of the shell pressed together and sticking up out of the sand.

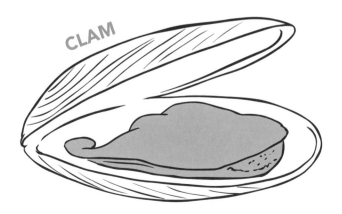

CLAM

Razor clams

Look for keyhole-shaped holes in the sand when there is a very low tide, pour some salt onto the hole and wait (quietly). The razor clam will pop up out of the sand so you can grab it (which might be the most fun thing to do on the beach ever!). Don't pull too hard or you'll tear them in half.

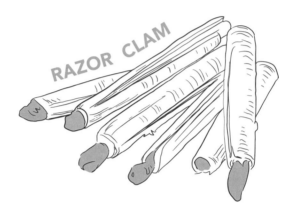

Prawns and shrimps

Catching prawns and shrimps is a beautiful way to spend an hour, an afternoon or the whole day. Affordable and basic nets are fine to use and will provide lots of fun and a good catch, but don't buy the very cheapest nets (they will fall apart in seconds).

Making your own net is a very, very good investment in your time. Choose a decent pole from the woods (hazel is perfect), shape a hoop or band of metal to create the frame of your net (a thick wire coat hanger can work for this) and lash it to your pole, and add your netting by attaching it to the metal hoop with wire (it'll last loads longer than cord). Netting can be made from onion sacks or bought cheaply online.

Hunt for prawns and shrimps in the shallows and rock pools where there are places for them to hide.

Prawns and shrimps should be steamed or boiled in salt water over a fire on the beach and then peeled and eaten immediately. They will taste sweet, a little salty and wonderful!

Crayfish

We think that freshwater crayfish deserve a special mention all on their own. Catching, cooking and eating crayfish can take up an entire wonderful weekend.

You're only allowed to catch 'non-native' crayfish in the UK and you need a licence from the environment agency to catch crayfish with traps (other methods are not restricted). The most common invasive species are American Signal Crayfish which are really easy to identify. Signal Crayfish are much larger than the 'white claw crayfish' that are native to the UK, and they also have a distinctive white/turquoise flash at the point where there pincers hinge. A few minutes on the internet will help you find out whether there are any streams, waterways or canals near you that have lots of invasive crayfish in them. The best time to hunt for crayfish is mid-spring to mid-autumn: they tend to go dormant and hibernate when the water gets too cold. Make sure you have permission from the landowner before you start any crayfish hunting adventures.

CRAYFISH

The most fun way to collect crayfish is to wade along a stream bed with a bucket and a net, or to catch them with a crab line.

To hunt them in a shallow stream slowly wade against the flow of the water (so you're walking upstream) and gently turn over any likely looking rocks. If you're lucky there will be a crayfish or two underneath, ready for you to scoop up in your net.

To catch them with a crab line use enticing bait (uncooked chicken drumsticks are cheap and work really well) and have your net ready to hold under the critters as you take them out of the water. You can catch hundreds of crayfish an hour with a crab line. Once you've found some good spots, mark them on a map and tell us where they are!

If you fancy having a go at catching crayfish with traps then licences are free and easy to get in some crayfish spots. Effective traps can be bought cheaply online; the 'spring' net traps are great as they compress really small but can catch a lot of crayfish. Bait your trap with chicken, cat food or tinned sardines and leave it in the water at least overnight. If there are crayfish about there will be some in the trap when you come back the next day.

Once you've caught crayfish and want to eat them it's best to remove the sand vein before or after cooking them. To remove the

66 You're only allowed to catch 'non-native' crayfish in the UK 99

sand vein before cooking gently pull the central fin of the crayfish straight backwards, it should detach bringing the sand vein away with it. If you've cooked your crayfish then a quick incision along the back of each peeled tail will alow you to remove the thin dark line.

To cook crayfish, simply add to salted boiling water and simmer for about 5 minutes. The crayfish will turn bright red. Let the wonderful beasts cool for a few minutes and then devour. They taste amazing, with the best meat coming from the tail and the chunky claws. Use scissors and even pliers to help get as much meat as possible from each crayfish. If you want to be really posh then take a lemon and some mayo next time you fancy cooking crayfish – they are wonderful dipped in lemon mayonnaise.

WHOLE FISH

Most fish tastes great when cooked over the fire and, best of all, it's really easy to do. You can get fish from the supermarket, fishmongers or (even better) catch it yourself. Some of the best fish to use, like mackerel and trout, is very, very tasty and cheap to buy.

If you catch your own or buy your fish completely intact you will need to gut and clean them, by cutting the stomach open with a sharp knife and using your fingers to scoop out the insides. If you're catching the fish yourself it's best to gut them where you caught them and return any waste back to the water.

Good fresh fish shouldn't smell very much; if your fish is a few days old and a bit pongy it's probably best to bin it or use it as bait.

" Good fresh fish shouldn't
smell strongly **"**

Things to try with whole fish

Try making foil parcels of a whole fish, seasoning, a squeeze of citrus fruit or some white wine. Wrap the contents well within the foil so no steam can escape and cook over a gentle fire for about half an hour (or less depending on the size of the fish), turning the parcels over every now and again. You can also bury the parcels in embers and leave for the same amount of time. Let everyone open their own fishy parcel and eat out of the foil to minimise the washing up. Tasty and faff free!

Trout and salmon can be gently separated from their bones until the whole fish can be laid flat and held over the fire using a splay, a simple cooking tool that holds your fish open while it cooks over the fire.

Cook gently and add a squeeze of lemon and some salt to finish. The fish will taste delicious and slightly smoky.

Any fish can be added to stews and soups. It cooks through really quickly and is great with chunks of crusty bread.

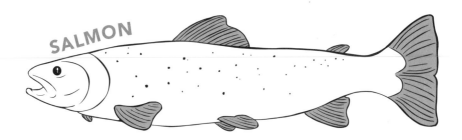

SALMON

NOTES

....
....
....
....
....
....
....
....
....
....
....
....
....
....
....
....

COOKING IN THE GREAT OUTDOORS

66 **Food prepared over a fire has that extra something that comes from cooking over coals, flames and woodsmoke** *99*

Preparing food and eating outdoors is a wonderful and life-affirming activity. Simply being in the fresh air adds a certain tasty something to each and every bite of the food you create, and the exertion and the extra effort put forth to create gastronomic delights in the great outdoors is a fantastic way to build up an appetite.

Eating food that you have prepared and cooked whilst sat around a fire that you have built with friends and family is, for many, the most enjoyable part of heading outside to enjoy bushcraft. Food prepared over a fire has that extra something that comes from cooking over coals, flames and woodsmoke.

Once you've tried cooking a few things over a fire you'll soon realise just how easy it can be, and we strongly recommend experimenting as much as you possibly can. There's loads of easily available inspiration for new recipe ideas and cooking techniques out there.

When you've experimented a little you'll be able to feed your tribe confidently with food that not only tastes great but is brilliant value and lots of fun to prepare and eat.

A few things that are really useful when cooking over an open fire:

Gardening or 'rigger' gloves – the perfect outdoor oven glove.

Extra-long tongs – fires can be really hot, and long tongs save your arm hair.

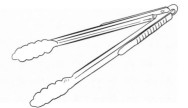

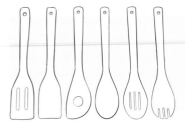

Wooden cooking tools – plastic tends to get a bit 'melty'.

MARSHMALLOWS

Why wouldn't you? Since the dawn of time (well, almost), men, women and children have been sharpening sticks, gathering around fires and toasting the humble marshmallow. The transformation from the rather dull and vaguely sweet combination of whipped sugar, corn starch and gelatine (veggie alternatives are available) to slightly charred, wonderfully browned, crispy, gooey, aromatic delight is staggering in its speed, simplicity and magnitude.

The best marshmallows to use are the archetypal white or pink kind that are about the same diameter as a fifty-pence piece. These usually come in large bags that can be bought almost anywhere (veggie ones tend to be more readily available online). Don't be tempted to buy the colourful, unnecessary and over-complicated versions; a true master of marshmallow toasting is a purist – simplicity of shape and colour are essential in obtaining the perfect finished article.

What you will need

Some marshmallows – We prefer white ones but all colours toast beautifully.

A fire – Let your fire burn down to brightly glowing coals.

Something to sit on – Brilliant toasted marshmallows take time; squatting can cause legs to ache and the job to be rushed. A suitable stump or log to sit on allows everyone to concentrate on the job in hand.

A sharpened stick – Something at least as long as your forearm and somewhere between a pencil and your little finger in thickness; sharpening a stick is a brilliant job by which to learn how to use a knife safely. Children sat around a fire with their elbows on their knees and under direct supervision will be able to safely fashion their own superb toasting tool.

Optional extras – Hot chocolate, wet wipes, wide open spaces for burning off the inevitable sugar rush.

TIP

For real luxury take a packet of your tribe's favourite biscuit and sandwich the molten marshmallow between two of those biscuits then enjoy. We strongly recommend a chocolate-coated, knobbly, oaty biscuit for this task.

What you should do

- Light a fire (see Fire chapter, page 30), and use the best wood you can find. Dry, quality wood will give you the best possible coals and great quality coals will give you the best possible toasted marshmallow. Let your fire burn down until there are few flames and lots of coals.

- Once you're sat around your brightly glowing embers with sharpened sticks, carefully insert the point through the very centre of your marshmallow. Accuracy is all – the ability to 'roll' your marshmallow for even cooking will give you brilliant results.

- Use your sharpened stick to hold your marshmallow a few centimetres from a likely looking area of glowing embers. Don't let it touch any part of the fire; subtle texture changes should be obtained by careful crisping and NOT by picking up great chunks of charred wood and grit.

- Slowly rotate your marshmallow over the embers, trying to give each side an even amount of cooking time and heat. It will start to bubble and brown as it cooks: keep rotating as this happens or you will overcook and char one side.

- A brilliant toasted marshmallow is one that is lightly browned all over with the occasional 'extra' cooked area for a little more flavour and texture.

- The outside of the marshmallow should be crisp, browned and blistered. The inside will be molten, gooey and HOT.

- Blow on your marshmallow and leave it to cool a little. Make sure that your tribe allow their marshmallows to cool: molten sugar stuck to your chin is hardly ever pleasant.

- Feast on sticky, warm, sugary, caramelised goodness!

TWIST BREAD

The simplest of recipes, lots and lots of fun, really easy to prepare and with loads of tasty ways to enjoy.

This is perhaps the easiest way of preparing bread over an open fire. It requires almost no equipment, cooks quickly, is tasty, fills up empty tummies and can be dipped in, served with or stuffed full of almost everything.

What you will need

Dough ingredients – Four good handfuls of flour, enough water to form a firm dough and a pinch of both salt and yeast or baking powder.

A bowl – To mix it all up in.

A fire – Let your fire burn down to a few flames with lots of brightly glowing coals.

Something to sit on – Cooking tasty twist bread takes time; something to sit on will help your tribe focus on the job in hand. Everything in the outdoors is more fun if you're comfortable.

A 'skinned' stick – Something at least as long as your arm from fingertip to shoulder and about as thick as your index finger. Remove all the bark from about a third of your stick and roll it through a flame for a few seconds to dry it out.

Optional extras – Soup, stew, jam, golden syrup, hot chocolate for dipping.

What you should do

- To make your dough, mix all the ingredients together, binding with just enough water to form dough which doesn't stick to your hands.

- Knead well and then leave to prove for a few minutes.

- You can either make your dough at home and transport it in a freezer bag or two or get everyone involved in mixing and kneading your dough while sat around your fire. You'll need to be able to wash everyone's hands after this has been done.

- Get a fire going using the best wood you can find; dry, seasoned 'hard' wood will give you really nice flames, embers and a good even heat to cook on once the fire has burnt down. It should only take about half an hour for your fire to burn down enough to give you a great cooking fire.

- Gather your tribe, give them a pre-skinned stick or help them skin their own.

- Distribute tennis ball-sized balls of dough; get everyone to roll the dough between their hands to form long snakes no thicker than your thumb.

- Twist the dough evenly onto your stick until your whole snake has been tightly coiled around your stick. Try not to leave gaps between your coils, your stick should look a little like a 'Twister' ice lolly.

- Once everyone has beautifully coiled dough, sit them around the fire and hold the coils of dough at least 10 cm away from your embers. Slowly rotate your coiled dough above the heat; a really careful rotation will give you the most even cooking and the best results.

- After a few minutes of cooking your twist will start to gently brown. Move it ever so slightly away from the heat and keep rotating; everyone should do their best to cook the middle of their dough really well without burning the outside of the twist.

- Rushing things will lead to a black, burnt outside and a raw, gooey inside which is, quite frankly, fairly disgusting to eat, even with golden syrup. After about 15 minutes of slow and even rotating your twist should be well browned and a little larger than when you started cooking.

- To test if your twist is done remove it from the heat, let it cool ever so slightly and gently tap the crust that has formed on the outside, the dough should sound hollow and feel lighter.

- A twist cooked to perfection should slide off the stick without leaving any sticky bits of dough behind. Once you're confident your bread is ready, slide it from the stick onto a plate, leaf or a clean stone to cool for a few minutes.

- Twist bread tastes great on its own; cooking the dough over an open fire gives it a wonderful, slightly smoky flavour that is beautifully primeval and satisfying. For some variety or to sweeten things up try a little jam, golden syrup or chocolate spread.

- Cooking twist bread is a great way of entertaining your tribe while you cook a main course, whatever it may be.

POPCORN

You don't need to take a trip to the cinema to enjoy popcorn; it's just as tasty (and much, much cheaper) to pop your own corn over an open fire.

Popcorn is very, very easy to make and can be sugared, salted, syruped, paprikaed or flavoured with pretty much anything you can think of. Corn for popping can be bought almost everywhere and is really good value. A little goes a long way.

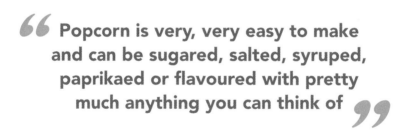

" Popcorn is very, very easy to make and can be sugared, salted, syruped, paprikaed or flavoured with pretty much anything you can think of "

What you will need

Corn – For popping

An old saucepan or 'billy' – With a lid

A little vegetable oil

A fire – As long as you have flames you should be able to pop your corn

Sugar/salt – Or whatever flavouring you fancy

Optional extras – Something to hang or rest your pot on **(see Making Things and Carving chapter, page 176)** can help make life easier.

What you should do

- Build a fire; it doesn't need to be huge but you'll need it to burn for 20 minutes or so and provide enough heat to pop your corn.

- Add enough oil to generously cover the bottom of the pan.

- Place your pan on the fire, on your grill or hang it from your pot hanger and leave it to heat up for a few minutes.

- When the pan is hot, but before the oil starts to smoke, carefully add enough popping corn to completely cover the base of your pan; don't be tempted to add more, a little goes a long way. Put the lid on your pan.

- Gently jiggle your pan every few seconds, remember that the pan will be very hot.

- When you hear your corn start popping DON'T take your lid off, keep jiggling. The noise emanating from your pan should now be evocative of line dancers on bubble wrap.

- When the popping noises have started to abate a little, keep jiggling and take your pan off the heat but leave the lid on.

- While gently jiggling, wait for all popping noises to cease, take the lid off your pan and amaze your tribe with your pan of pale, fluffy, beautifully popped corn.

- Add sugar, salt or whatever else you fancy. Enjoy!

STEWS, SOUPS AND OTHER ONE-PAN WONDERS

Anything that you can cook on a hob indoors can be cooked above an open fire.

What you will need

A fire – with enough wood to cook your meal; four or five good armfuls of wood should be enough – don't wait until it has run out before you collect some more.

A Dutch oven – A billy can or an old saucepan with a lid

Something to hang your pan from – Or something to rest your pan on

Plates and cutlery – Or mugs and spoons

Optional extras – A tea towel, a pair of gardening gloves or anything else that will help you move hot pans.

What you should do

Option 1
- Cook a 'one pot' meal at home; stews, soups, chillies and curries all work really well.

- Once your meal has cooled decant it into a large freezer bag or reusable plastic containers and store it in the fridge until you're ready to leave.

- Carry your pre-prepared food to your favourite fire spot.

- Light a fire, transfer the meal to your cooking pot of choice and slowly, gently heat the food through.

- Serve it with great chunks of crusty bread (or twist bread that you make while you're waiting for the stew to heat up).

- Enamel mugs that hold a pint are perfect for serving your food into and have the added benefit that your tribe can warm their hands at the same time that they warm their tummies. Just make sure nobody burns their hands!

Option 2
- Get your fire going, then let it burn down a little until you have a decent bed of embers and good consistent heat.

- Make sure you have enough wood on hand to maintain your fire for as long as you need.

- Position your pan above your fire and let it warm up.

- Chop your ingredients directly into the pan, stirring occasionally.

- Add enough liquid to cover (you really, really don't want the bottom of your dinner to burn) and leave to cook with the lid on.

- Once cooked serve as per option 1.

OUR SIMPLE 'CAMP STEW'

Take some chunks of meat, roughly chopped onions, chunks of root veg (sweet potatoes and carrots are great), a jar of blackcurrant jam, stock cubes or pots, a bunch of any fresh herbs you can find, add water to cover and leave to cook with the lid on.

STEAK

A steak is a treat; a steak seared on an open fire is doubly so. Once you've mastered creating great fires for cooking upon, treat the tribe to a tremendous meaty treat.

What you will need

Your favourite cut of steak – Rump or sirloin is great, but our favourite is rib-eye. If you'd like something a little different then try some venison: loin or haunch steaks are great on the fire.

A really, really good fire – Fuelled with the best possible dry, seasoned wood split into good lengths.

A clean fire grill – An old BBQ grill works fine.

Olive oil and seasoning.

What you should do

- Build a fire: use the best wood you can find, let your fire develop until you have a great bed of really hot coals. Don't be stingy with the fuel.
- Apply olive oil and seasoning to your steaks.
- Place the steaks down onto your grill above the hottest part of your fire and leave them for a few minutes before turning onto the flip side.
- Leave your steaks to rest on a much cooler section of the fire grill or on a plate next to the fire – you want them to stay warm but not cook any more.
- Salivate. Eat your steak – it will be delicious.

NOTES

....
....
....
....
....
....
....
....
....
....
....
....
....
....
....
....
....

NOTES

STAYING OUT
OVERNIGHT

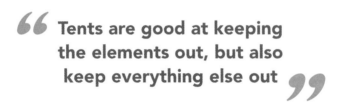

**" Tents are good at keeping
the elements out, but also
keep everything else out "**

Sleeping outside is excellent fun.

Our definition of sleeping outside is having at least part of whatever shelter you choose completely open to allow you to enjoy the great outdoors all night long.

Tents are good at keeping the elements out, but also keep everything else out; the stars, the breeze, the drifting smell of woodsmoke – all the things that are wonderful about sleeping in the woods.

On a warm summer's evening there is absolutely no reason why you shouldn't sleep out in the open. A tarp or roll mat to lie on and a sleeping bag or blanket to sleep under are all that you need. If you can find a small clearing in the woods to sleep in you'll get the best of both worlds – stars to look at and trees to listen to.

Journeying to and finding the place you are going to camp, building a fire and preparing the area, cooking your evening meal, toasting marshmallows and making hot drinks are all part of an experience which speaks to something primeval within all of us.

Staying out at night doesn't have to be stressful and scary. You can start in a tent in the back garden where showers, toilets and everything else you need are still close at hand.

From the back garden it's easy to progress to a campsite and from there you're only a step away from staying a night in the woods.

REMEMBER: ALWAYS GET PERMISSION FROM THE LANDOWNER IF AT ALL POSSIBLE

THINGS TO CONSIDER

TOILETS

There aren't likely to be any toilets close enough for you to use in the woods. You will need to wee in the great outdoors and you may need to do a poo.

Weeing in the woods is easy; walk at least 20 paces from where you're camping and find a convenient tree or bush to wee against or behind. If you intend to use a site often you might want to walk further.

Pooing in the woods could be considered to be a little more complex. There are people that think it's really important to carry everything you carried into the woods back out with you, especially if the area is used by lots of people. This means bagging and storing poo until you get back to civilisation; a combo of dog poo bags and decent freezer bags works for this.

Some people think that taking a trowel and digging a small but relatively deep hole is the best way to relieve yourself outdoors. Poo in the hole, wipe your bum then bury everything under a good layer of earth.

Some people think that that burying poo and paper means that it often decomposes more slowly than leaving it exposed.

We think that walking a good distance from your camp, footpaths, or water sources and finding a good tree to lean up against is the most comfortable way to poo in the woods. Dig a hole if you think it best, or at least have some leaf litter ready to cover up your poo when you have finished. Wipe your bum with loo roll then very carefully burn it with a gas lighter or some matches (the loo roll, not your bum). Some of your tribe might be a bit young to safely burn their own paper; paper bags are great for bagging it to be burned or binned later. If you fancy a really clean bum consider a last polish with a wet wipe which you can either bag and carry out or burn on your fire.

Poo in general

If you're planning your first poo in the woods or on a hillside then make it a good one and consider your diet in the days running up to your camping trip. We recommend a diet rich in fibre and staying well hydrated for at least two days before you set off.

When you arrive at your campsite consider where will be best to enjoy your poo, scout around and find an area that has a nice view or will have a clear view of the night sky later. You might like to dig your hole now as well.

When the time comes, relax, get comfortable and enjoy every last moment of the wonderful, primeval experience that pooing outdoors is.

SHELTER

Choose or make a shelter that is appropriate for you, your tribe, the conditions and the location. There is little point in building a huge thatched shelter for a single dry night out in the woods. While building the shelter can be great fun and a good learning experience, you'll also be using up lots of the area's resources without good reason.

You and your tribe need to be safe and comfortable. In the summer that might mean a couple of blankets next to your cooking fire, in the winter being safe and comfortable probably means you'll have to build substantial shelters, robust fires and lots of mats, blankets and/or sleeping bags.

It's quick and easy to make a bed more comfortable than the ground; a good thickness of vegetation will provide great insulation and make you much more cosy. If you fancy building something more substantial lash a bed 'frame' together from lengths of timber and fill with vegetation.

Whatever you decide to do, always remove any trace of your camp the next morning; other people wanting to enjoy the wild, unspoilt woods will not appreciate stumbling upon the remains of your camp.

WATER

For most single night camps the easiest and least troublesome method of obtaining water is simply to carry it with you. A couple of litres for each member of your group is more than enough to drink and cook with overnight. Collecting, storing and making water safe to drink is a complex procedure. If you're lucky enough to be somewhere in the UK where you are confident to drink water out of streams and rivers then that's great. The only sources we feel confident to drink water from without treating it are fast flowing streams high up in remote wilderness areas.

If you're not confident then be very wary; water can carry all sorts of hidden dangers which can originate from human or animal waste, pesticides, rotting animal life and all manner of less than lovely sources (see the Water chapter, page 47).

FOOD

'Wild' camping will normally mean a journey, lots of time outdoors, being really active and keeping as warm as possible.

Always expect to need a little more food than you think. It's best to base your afternoon and evening around where the next meal, snack or drink is coming from.

Cooking and eating is something that will bring everyone together around the fire. Involve as many people in preparing food as possible.

Make sure that people keep their hands and utensils clean; hygiene is really important to prevent upset tummies.

Plan your meals and consider doing some of the preparation work at home. For example, chopping onions in the woods is a nuisance, it's far easier to chop them at home and bag them up to add to your stew when they are needed.

As well as the staple meals of lunch, breakfast and dinner which should be tasty, warming and filling, make sure you plan for lots of snacks and treats. Your tribe will have an excellent time making twist bread or toasting marshmallows and will also have an energy-laden snack as a result.

Eating healthy food is really important but there is no doubt that, when you're exploring the great outdoors, you burn loads more energy than usual. It's really important to make sure that everyone gets the calories they need to stay warm and happy. Healthy, calorie-rich snacks include bananas, dried fruit, jerky and nuts. The occasional chunk of chocolate is really good for keeping energy levels up.

ACTIVITIES

Preparing your camp, cooking lovely food and going for a poo are certainly going to take up some of the afternoon and evening but it's brilliant to have a few activities up your sleeve to keep everyone entertained. A foraging walk can add a few lush ingredients for dinner and making spoons will provide the utensils (though it's worth taking a few backups). Wildlife watching, hunting and tracking are all fantastic things to do as the sun starts to go down and lots of creatures become more active.

 Wildlife watching, hunting and tracking are all fantastic things to do as the sun starts to go down and lots of creatures become more active

NOTES

....

....

....

....

....

....

....

....

....

....

....

....

....

....

....

....

....

NOTES

TRACKING

 Animals give us lots of clues that let us know where they've been 🙶

Most animals and birds in the UK are crafty. Generally, if you're out for a walk in the woods they will hear you coming long before you'll ever set eyes on them and they'll head in the opposite direction.

The best way to see some of our awesome fauna, when you're out and about is to keep your eyes open and look for signs that animals have been in the same places as you.

Animals give us lots of clues that let us know where they've been. Keep your eyes, ears, nose and brain alert and they can be quite easy to spot. Look for footprints, poo and broken vegetation; listen for the crash of deer through the undergrowth or the squeaky bark of a squirrel overhead; sniff them out – some predators tend to wee and poo in the same places to mark their territory, which can all be a bit smelly. Marks on trees and tufts of fur caught on fences or branches are also clues that animals have visited somewhere.

Once you've realised that you're sharing your favourite places to walk, camp and play with animals, you can do your best to get close enough to watch them.

We don't have any natural predators in the UK but it's best to give all animals enough distance so you can watch them without disturbing them, as some animals can act aggressively or bolt if they feel threatened or trapped. Not only can you put yourself at risk if an animal displays such behaviour, but the animal can end up harming itself in an attempt to flee.

Stags can be completely unafraid of people and dogs and during the rut (the breeding season), which happens in the autumn, they can be really aggressive. Give them space to get on with their business by watching from a distance, with some binoculars if you have them. Listen out for them too, deer make weird and wonderful noises during the rut; woods and valleys can sound like something from *Jurassic Park*.

Binoculars and a camera are great tools to help with tracking and watching animals, taking pictures of animal signs, especially poo, can help you work out just which creatures are about and when they are visiting.

ANIMAL SIGNS

If the ground is soft, wet, sandy or snowy then you're likely to find the footprints of lots of the animals that have visited a place before you. Footprints can be very distinctive and tell you what the animal is, what it's doing and who it's with. Some animal tracks are very distinctive and common in the UK.

Animal poo can be very, very useful in letting you know which species have been in the vicinity. Most herbivore poo from wild animals in the UK will consist of 'droppings' of different sizes that are clearly made up of digested vegetable matter. Rabbits and deer have similar diets so their poo looks similar. The difference lies in the size of the droppings – deer poo is larger.

Poo from carnivores (foxes) and omnivores (badgers) can be a bit more varied but will usually look like a poo from a small dog. What sets the poo apart from that of a dog can be traces of fur and fine feathers within it. The fur in predator poo often helps it to form a point as it leaves the animal's bottom.

Poo can tell you even more than footprints; it's wonderful stuff for the tracker. Poo can tell you how long it's been since the animal was present, for instance fresh poo might even be warm. We don't recommend touching poo, it can contain parasites and nasty bacteria.

Animals leave lots of evidence other than poo to let us know when they've been around. Their feeding habits are a good way of revealing their presence. Herbivores will often leave cropped plants, stripped bark or scrapes in snow. Check stumps of trees for piles of nut and pine cone detritus left by squirrels; in winter look out for discarded acorn shells or nibbled tree shoots and small branches to see if deer have been around.

A pile of feathers usually marks where a predator has made a kill then carried its food away to eat in private. Skulls and the larger bones are often all that remain of animals that have been killed by predators; if you find these check them for teeth marks.

DEER

If you're a little distant from built-up areas, in the woods, around the edges of fields, following a footpath, or on heathland, then you're likely to see deer tracks, or 'slots' as they're known. Deer tracks are really distinctive: they have two 'toes' (slots) that are close together which look a bit like an upside-down 'heart' shape.

The narrow end of the track points towards the direction the deer was moving in. The larger the track, the bigger the deer; this might depend on the age or the species of the animal. Most areas of the UK have an abundance of deer and there are usually several species living on the same area. Deer tracks from different species are difficult to tell apart based on shape.

DEER

If you find a place with lots of deer tracks it's worth trying to approach the area quietly. If you walk into the wind (so the deer can't smell you) next time you visit, you stand a good chance of spotting deer and even getting quite close. The best time of day to see deer is early in the morning or late in the evening.

Deer poo is made up of droppings that are bigger but very similar to rabbit droppings. Most species in the UK will leave clumps of droppings that are individually the same size as a marble. You'll usually be able to make out what the deer had for its dinner by looking closely at the poo; grass is most common but you can also find acorn and chestnut shells. Deer poo a lot (normally up to 15 times a day).

Deer leave other quite recognisable signs of their presence: stags will often scratch and scrape themselves and their antlers on trees leaving clear marks in the bark; they often feed in the same areas day to day and these regular visits create distinct tracks and obvious clearings through woodland and hedges. Deer will lie down to rest up or sleep when they are not feeding; if you look carefully their 'beds' can be clearly seen in the shape of patches of flattened-down vegetation on the forest floor or in the undergrowth bordering fields.

LARGISH PREDATORS

We've done a good (or terrible) job of killing off most of the predator species in the UK and, sadly, bears, wolves and lynx no longer roam our island.

Badger

Stoat

Fox

Weasel

Mink

Our common predator species living in the wild are now the fox, badger, weasel, mink and stoat. You might be lucky enough to see wild cat tracks in the more remote parts of Scotland and otters are making a comeback in many areas of the UK as well.

There are fewer predators than plant eaters and they tend to be a bit more reclusive. You're much more likely to see a fox in a town than in the woods these days.

fox

The most commonly seen predators are badgers and foxes and they identify themselves easily with some clear traces. Paw prints are the most common and are

badger

similar but distinct enough to tell apart; fox prints are really similar to dog prints with four toe indentations that sit forward of the main pad with the front two toes noticeably forward of the back two. Badger prints are made up of five toe indentations that lie in a curved line in front of the main pad.

Predator (or carnivore) poo can be a bit more varied than herbivore poo and will often be splat, coil or cigar shaped. It will often contain fur, feathers or small bones – elements of a predator's diet that do not digest. Poo with a lot of hair in it is easy to identify as it will be pointed at one end and visibly hairy.

Predators can be choosy about where they sleep, and the homes they make give us great clues to which animal is in the vicinity. For instance, badgers are brilliant at digging and live in tunnels called setts. Setts are amazing things and can be home to lots of generations of badger families for hundreds of years. The extensive network of tunnels that comprise a sett can go on for hundreds of metres in woodlands or hedgerows. To find a sett look for large, badger-sized holes in quiet woodland or countryside; badger holes are usually wider than they are tall and about 30 cm in diameter. The ground around the hole will be free of undergrowth and there will be badger tracks in any loose or wet soil.

Badger setts are the best places to see badgers on a moonlit night or in the late evening; sit quietly downwind and far enough away from the badgers that you won't disturb them. Badgers have very good hearing and a superb sense of smell; if you rustle or wear aftershave they won't come anywhere near you.

Foxes sometimes sleep in dens but are more likely to sleep curled up in dense undergrowth – it's really hard to spot where foxes have been sleeping.

RABBITS

Keeping your eyes peeled and your ears open is the best way to find smaller critters. Walking quietly into the wind is essential and creeping up a bank or ridge to see what's on the other side is a great technique.

It can be easy to spot where rabbits have been. Look for:

Burrows – Lots of small (rabbit-sized) openings in a hedgerow or bank. Any openings that are in use will be clear of vegetation and have rabbit poo close by.

Poo – Think raisins that have gone a bit off and turned a little green.

Tracks – Rabbit feet are furry and don't leave very distinct foot prints. The illustration to the right shows what to look out for.

Grazing – There will signs of grazing, i.e. cropped grass and other vegetation, near rabbit burrows. Often strips of crops next to hedges will be completely devoured by rabbits.

rabbit

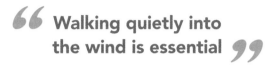

Walking quietly into the wind is essential

SQUIRRELS

Squirrels can be easy to see once the leaves have fallen from the trees. Before then you may well hear them rustling, chattering and barking in the canopy.

The easiest way to see where they have been is to look for nut and pine cone detritus on tree stumps, rocks or other flat surfaces.

Squirrel poo is small, brown and hard to spot. It looks a bit like big, brown grains of rice.

BIRDS

There are hundreds of species of birds in the UK, and we can't possibly talk about them all. We've mentioned the basics; there are lots and lots of books on birds if you fancy a bit more information.

Bird tracks are really easy to spot and most of them look really similar but vary in size. Most birds have four toes, with three facing forward and one facing back.

Most people can spot bird poo. Watch out for colour changes with the seasons. When blackberries are out lots of bird poo will turn purple.

Bird nests are easy to spot in the autumn. If you spot lots of bird poo on the ground underneath a tree look up; you may well see a nest.

Keep an eye out for raptor pellets; any predatory bird will cough up these collections of bones, beaks, feathers and fur. Generally speaking the larger the bird the larger the pellet. If you find a pellet, break it open and see what it's made of – pellets aren't pooed out and are clean and not smelly.

If you're quiet and observant you may be lucky enough to see a raptor strike or come across it feeding. Keep your distance and get some pictures if you can. If you come across a small patch of scattered feathers in a field or other open ground then it's likely that a raptor has been feeding at that spot.

Pigeons can be easy to spot, especially in the autumn and spring when they come down to feed on newly ploughed or planted fields or head into leafless trees in the early evening. Wood pigeons and doves are very tasty and are designated a pest in the UK; if you have permission from the landowner it's fine to hunt these birds with the appropriate tools.

" If you come across a small patch of scattered feathers in a field or other open ground then it's likely that a raptor has been feeding at that spot "

NOTES

....
....
....
....
....
....
....
....
....
....
....
....
....
....
....
....

NATURAL NAVIGATION

66 A compass is a great tool to help you experiment with natural navigation **99**

People have navigated by nature for thousands of years. Be it sailors using the stars or Native Americans following herds of buffalo, it is possible to find your way without modern technology. It is also a great activity to do as a family as everyone can get involved and it's free!

You will not need any equipment so it's great to have a go at when you're out walking the dog or on your way to the park. Once you find that you are getting the hang of it you can then start setting yourself little challenges, but more on those later.

A compass is a great tool to help you experiment with natural navigation; they're not expensive to buy and are great to fall back on should you get a little lost. Compasses are easy to use – just remember that the big red arrow always points north.

SO WHAT CAN BE USED?

Let's start with the sun. The sun rises in the east right? Well yes – kind of. It only rises due east on the equinoxes (around 20 March and 22 September). An equinox is when the sun passes over the equator and the day and night are both 12 hours long. They also mark the beginning of spring and autumn. On the summer solstice (21 June in the Northern Hemisphere), it rises in the north-east and on the winter solstice (21 December), it rises in the south-east. So depending on what time of the year it is when you're doing this will mean you will have to adjust for the sun.

TIP

Here are two examples of natural navigation:

On the first day of spring (around 20 March) you are out walking the dog at sunrise. You are walking towards the sun so you are heading east. If you were walking away from the sun you would be heading west.

In midsummer at sunrise you are walking towards the sun. So you are heading north-east. Walking away from the sun you would be heading south-west.

For this method to work you need to know what time of the year it is and when the equinoxes or solstices are. But what if you don't? If in doubt grab a stick!

SHADOW STICK

What you will need

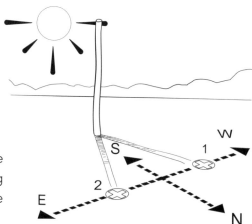

- A long stick
- The sun

What you should do

By using a stick it is possible to find your direction using the shadow cast from the sun.

Place a straight stick in to the ground. Make sure your stick is about a metre long to keep it simple and hassle free. The sun will now cast a shadow of the stick.

Mark the end of the shadow with a stone. This becomes your **WEST** point.

Wait 15 to 30 minutes. As the earth rotates around the sun the shadow will move. The longer you are able to wait the better.

Now mark the shadow again and this will become your **EAST** point. You will now have your east-west line. If you stand on your east-west line with west on your left and east on your right you are looking north. Simple!

Get the kids to give this a try so you can see if they managed to get it right. You can check either by using a compass or your phone – most phones have a compass app built in.

That's the sun then, but what happens if the sun's not out to play? Well that's not a problem – we will just use the trees and plants.

TREE AND MOSS GROWTH

What you will need

- Lone tree out in the open

What you should do

Trees love the light; it's how they grow. They use the energy from the sun, – they can't get enough of it – they seek it out, so we are able to use this to find a general direction.

The rule of thumb is the side of the tree with the most growth will indicate south.

The north side will have less growth and the growth it has will be trying to push upwards and towards the sun's rays. This works best on trees out in the open. Trees in woodland will tend to grow straight up to get the most light.

So if trees tend to grow towards the sunny south, what likes the cold damp north?

Moss, that's what!

You will notice that moss will be growing on the north sides of tree trunks and rocks. By combining these two gems of knowledge you are able to find your north-south line and once you know that you can figure out your east-west line as well.

Give it a go! Remember, the more trees you can find leaning towards the sun and the more moss patches you find hiding in the shade of the tree, the better your chances of finding a good strong indicator of north and south.

WATCH METHOD

What you will need

- Sun
- Analogue watch

What you should do

You can also use an analogue watch as a compass. This is a great little activity for the kids to try, as nothing can go wrong. The only equipment you need to check that they are right is a real compass.

If you are in the northern hemisphere lay the watch flat and face up in your palm, making sure the face is parallel with the ground.

Point the hour hand, and yourself, in the direction of the sun. It does not matter what the time is as long as it is accurate. Now all you need to do is bisect the angle between the 12 o'clock mark and the hour hand. This will give you a **south–north** line.

In the southern hemisphere you will need to point the 12 o'clock mark at the sun rather than the hour hand. This will give you a **north–south** line.

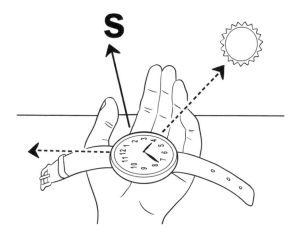

NIGHT-TIME NAVIGATION

This is all about using the stars and moon. Sailors have been doing this for hundreds of years and it still works today.

STARS

What you will need

- Clear night sky

What you should do

You are going to need to identify the Plough. The Plough consists of seven stars and looks like a large pan; you may know it as the Big Dipper. It is actually part of the Ursa Major (Great Bear) constellation. It is what is called an asterism, the name given to interesting and easily recognisable star patterns. So how do we use the Plough to help us find our way?

Once you've identified the Plough, locate the last two stars that form the pan section and follow them upward in a straight line by four times their own distance and you will have found Polaris (the North Star). This star sits directly over the North Pole. So, if you are walking towards it, guess what? You're heading north.

MOON

What you will need

- Crescent moon

What you should do

This only works on a crescent moon. All you need to do is draw a straight line down from the top part of the crescent to the bottom point and follow that line to the horizon. Where you hit the horizon, you'll have found south.

Try using the stars and moon to give you a very good indication of north and south and test it with a compass to see if you have got it right.

When you're out stargazing keep an eye out for the International Space Station. It looks like a very bright star moving across the sky. It will be moving faster than a plane and does not have any red or green lights. Looking through a telescope or binoculars it is possible to make out the shape of the solar panels. Not strictly bushcraft but cool never the less!

NOTES

....

....

....

....

....

....

....

....

....

....

....

....

....

....

....

....

NOTES

....

....

....

....

....

....

....

....

....

....

....

....

....

....

....

....

....

....

....

MAKING THINGS AND CARVING

Lots of people spend lots of money on shiny equipment to take with them into the woods or countryside. There's absolutely nothing wrong with shiny new equipment but buying it can get very, very expensive.

To make the things in this chapter you will need:

Knife – A sharp knife. Mora Clippers are great

Saw – Folding Baco Laplander or small pruning saw

A crook knife – For spoons and cups

Sandpaper

CROOK KNIFE

There is something fantastic about spending time outdoors making something that will last you, or someone else, a very long time.

There's not much that you can make from wood or other natural materials that is quick and easy to finish. Don't be put off though, not everything in life is quick and easy, and taking the time to create something functional or beautiful (or both) is deeply satisfying – the practice required to make really good stuff is rewarding.

Once you've practised a few techniques you'll be able to transfer those skills to make loads of different stuff.

The cord you use to help you make things can be bought or made but once you've practised on a few things we think it's a brilliant idea to create something from start to finish. There is a huge satisfaction in creating something with just your hands, natural materials and a knife.

TIP

It's worth learning to tie a few knots really well before you head out into the woods to explore, camp or make anything. Some of the best knots to learn are:

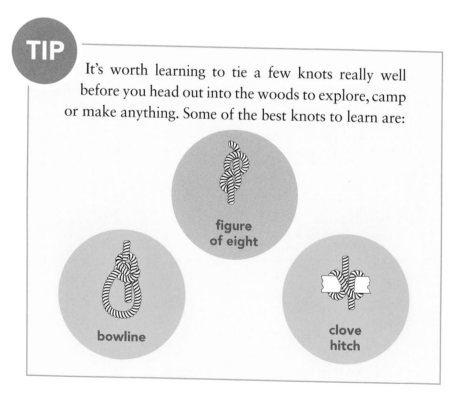

figure
of eight

bowline

clove
hitch

CARVING

There is something very addictive about working with wood while sitting round a campfire. It's great to whittle away the evening making whatever you and your hands feel like, with bellies full of good food and a warming drink on the go. We love it.

From the humble tent peg to a perfectly hollowed bowl and from spoons to hunting spears, carving allows you to make useful items whist out in the woods and also gives you something to take away with you at the end of your adventure.

Of course you don't have to be in the woods; you could just as easily head into the garden and get your carve on. That's the beauty and the appeal of it – grab your knife, find some wood and go at it.

Green wood (wood that is still alive, i.e. freshly cut) can be the best to work with, especially for a beginner, as it still has loads of moisture within it which makes it easy to use. Green hazel, ash or birch are great to start with.

The idea of letting your tribe loose with knives might fill you with dread, but don't be put you off. Sit them down, keep a close eye and trust them. Once they build up confidence and are firm but relaxed using the knife they will be safe, happy and enthralled.

Get them started with something small.

TENT PEG

The humble tent peg is essential when camping and is easy to make, allowing you to gain confidence and build up your carving skills. A nice set of hand-carved tent pegs is a brilliant and quick way to start carving. Once you have learned how to make them you can ditch the bent, twisted metal pegs that everyone struggles with, and travel a bit lighter.

What you will need

- Knife
- Saw
- A green 20 cm 'thumb-thick stick' – hazel is great for this

What you should do

- Find a green, straight stick and sharpen one end so you have a nice tapered point on it. This is the bit that goes in to the ground.

- Use a saw on the unsharpened end approximately 5 cm from the top. Saw into the stick roughly a quarter of the way through. This is known as a stop cut and will stop you from cutting too much off with your knife.

- Next, get your knife and slice at a 45-degree angle from underneath the stop cut to create a notch that will be able to hold a guy line.

- Now round off the top of the peg so when you hit it in the ground it won't split.

- Voila, you have just made your first tent peg.

Once everyone is happy with making tent pegs, have a go with different woods and see which everyone prefers and what works best for them.

TIP
Remove the bark from the peg and use a fire to harden the point to make it even stronger. Keep an eye on your pegs – you only want to char the tips.

A POT HANGER

To create a simple pot hanger, take two-forked sticks 50–70 cm long and bash them into the ground either side of your fire – make sure you leave enough space so they don't catch fire!

Take a sturdy green stick about as thick as your wrist and place in on to the forks so that it is held above the fire.

You can thread the stick through pot handles or use cord to hang your pots above the fire.

SPOON

You're going to need to eat with something.

Once you're happy with the way things are going and you feel the tribe are up to it, it's time to have a go at making a spoon. We love carving spoons: they can be very pretty and a great souvenir to take away from the woods with you. I will always write on the back of the handle, where, when and what wood I used. You do tend to build up a bit of a collection after a while. Spoons are brilliant presents for friends and family; everyone loves getting a present that has taken time, thought and skill.

What you will need

- Pencil or pen
- Knife
- Saw
- Sandpaper
- Crook knife
- Wood – Wrist thick, knot-free and green

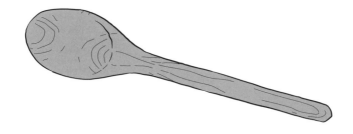

What you should do

- Split the wood down the middle and then split in half again so you are left with a floorboard-thickness bit of wood; 3 cm thick is about right.

- Draw the rough shape of a spoon on the wood.

- Take a saw and cut into the wood just under the bowl of the spoon.

- These are now your stop cuts. Whittle away, taking small amounts of wood off at a time. Remember you can take it off but you can't put it back on!

- Take your time and enjoy, it's not a race. Your thumbs may ache but it's definitely a 'good' ache.

- Once you have roughed out your spoon, start to shape the bowl. Carve away at the edges to start to curve the bottom of the spoon; once you're happy with the shape you have two choices -

Crook knife

Using a crook knife you can remove the top side of the spoon by scooping the wood out. Be sure not to cut your thumb when you're doing this, as you may be cutting towards it. Imagine you are trying to scoop ice cream from a tub. Don't get carried away and remove too much as you run the risk of turning your spoon into a sieve.

Ember

Take an ember from your fire and place it in a small dent in the top of the spoon – you can make the dent with the tip of your knife. Pinch the ember with a twig and gently blow.

This will start to burn away the bowl for your spoon. Once you are happy with the depth and look, remove the ember and scrape away the scorch marks and sand to a nice smooth finish.

You can always apply a little oil to the completed spoon to protect it and bring out the grain; walnut or hazelnut works extremely well.

You can also use the ember technique to carve a cup.

CUP

What you will need

- A dry, dead, solid log – About the thickness of a large mug
- Knife
- Water
- Sandpaper

What you should do

- Find a suitable bit of wood – oak or ash work really well.
- Using your knife remove the outer bark and carve in a small hole in the top.
- Apply your ember just like the spoon and blow gently.
- Add more embers when you need them and continue to burn out the mug.
- Every now and then scrape out the mug and start again.
- Once you're happy with your mug, plunge it into water to put the ember out, scrape off the charcoal and sand the inside down.
- Clean the mug and apply a little oil to seal it.

Once you have mastered these techniques, try making bowls in the same way, or have a go at making a cheese board, chopping board or whatever else you fancy – just take your time and enjoy yourself. The first things you make might not be perfect or pretty but the time spent working with wood as a family around the fire is what matters.

NOTES

....
....
....
....
....
....
....
....
....
....
....
....
....
....
....
....

NOTES

....

....

....

....

....

....

....

....

....

....

....

....

....

....

....

....

....

LEAVING NO TRACE

❝ Always endeavour to teach others to look after the countryside ❞

Enjoy the great outdoors whenever and wherever you can.

Never miss an opportunity to get out in the wilderness, woods or countryside, but do everything you can to minimise your impact on the landscapes you enjoy.

Dropping or leaving litter is inexcusable, perhaps one of the worst things you could ever do while enjoying the outdoors. Not only does litter leave a blight on the landscape, it can be smelly, it has the potential to harm animals and it can be toxic to ecosystems. Some litter, like paper and card, can be safely burnt on a campfire but most will have to be carried away with you and disposed of properly.

If you build anything in the woods – a shelter, an archery target, a practice trap or a fire – then you must make sure that once you leave there is no evidence that you were ever there.

Fires must be completely extinguished. Let them burn out, then use water to finish the job; there can be no trace of heat whatsoever left in any fire debris. If you've been efficient with your fuel then this shouldn't be much of a problem – we find it's only the really big (unnecessary) fires that are a pain to put out. Once a fire is out remove any leftover debris, such as ash or small pieces of charcoal, to somewhere very inconspicuous. Next, distribute leaf litter or soil to cover your fire area; anyone walking past somewhere you've lit a fire shouldn't realise that anything has been burnt in the vicinity.

If you find evidence that other people have been through an area, like rubbish or shelters that are still in situ, do you best to reduce the visibility and impact of other people's use (tidy up after other people).

Consider the manner in which you transport food and drink outdoors. Think about your use of 'disposable' items, e.g. some people think glow sticks are fun but they are single use, made of plastic, have lots of packaging and contain chemicals – is all that harm really worth four hours of feeble light?

Buy or make trail and camp food that has very little or no packaging, use reusable containers rather than freezer bags for storage, and try to think about how you can have the least impact on the environment with your actions and what you use. Consider the amount of natural resources available to you when you are in the wild. Many of the activities related to bushcraft draw on what's naturally available, such as burning dead wood, cutting live wood for tools, utilising bark from fallen trees and using ferns or vegetation for cord, shelters, bedding or fire; if you plunder the spot you're in and use up all these resources there won't be any left for others.

Cutting live wood is sometimes necessary; any growth should be removed in such a way that it affects the tree as little as possible. By being selective and considerate about the growth you remove you can actually make the tree healthier – consider the location, direction and visibility of your cuts. Never take too much growth from a single tree, try to cut branches from denser areas of growth and angle your cuts to allow water to run off the tree, away from the main growth.

As a guide, if someone visiting an area after you've used it could tell that you've been there, e.g. if large areas of ferns have been cut, if lots of hazel has been taken or if all the fallen wood has been burnt then you've had too much impact.

Give something back. If you visit an area regularly then arrange a trip just to look after that special place. We're based down in Dorset and often visit our beaches and woodland to litter pick for a few hours.

If any part of the landscape you visit is managed by volunteers, a charity or local people, consider giving up some of your time to help them. An understanding of the work that goes into maintaining the countryside will give you a greater connection to the landscape.

If you see or hear about anyone using an area badly then make sure you tell them why what they're doing is wrong. Do your best to challenge their actions and lack of consideration; take the responsibility and always endeavour to teach others to look after the countryside.

66 If we all look after and think about doing our bit to preserve our right to enjoy the landscapes that provide us with so much fulfilment, joy and shared experience, we can ensure they'll still be here for future generations to use 99

Consider how you journey into the landscapes you visit when enjoying the great outdoors. If you don't need to drive then please, please don't. Visiting an area on foot, by bike or by using public transport reduces your impact on an area and is much more discreet.

The UK is one of the most densely populated countries in the world; there are 65 million people living on an island with only a small amount of space that can be used for outdoor activities. We must look after the spaces we do have. If you feel as passionately about the countryside as we do, why not fight for more spaces to be made available to us and join in campaigns to resist any individual, organisation or legislation that makes it harder for the public to enjoy the great outdoors.

If we all look after and think about doing our bit to preserve our right to enjoy the landscapes that provide us with so much fulfilment, joy and shared experience, we can ensure they'll still be here for future generations to use.

NOTES

....
....
....
....
....
....
....
....
....
....
....
....
....
....
....
....

If you're interested in finding out more about our books,
find us on Facebook at **Summersdale Publishers**
and follow us on Twitter at **@Summersdale**.

www.summersdale.com